W9-BJJ-642

*Wordsmithery*

# Wordsmithery

## A Guide to Working at Writing

### Second Edition

Robert L. Root, Jr.
*Central Michigan University*

**Allyn and Bacon**

BOSTON ▪ LONDON ▪ TORONTO ▪ SYDNEY ▪ TOKYO ▪ SINGAPORE

*Executive Editor:* Eben W. Ludlow
*Editorial Assistant:* Linda D'Angelo
*Marketing Manager:* Lisa Kimball
*Editorial-Production Administrator:* Rob Lawson
*Editorial-Production Service:* Omegatype Typography, Inc.
*Composition Buyer:* Linda Cox
*Manufacturing Buyer:* Suzanne Lareau
*Text Design:* Omegatype Typography, Inc.
*Cover Administrator:* Jenny Hart

Copyright © 1998 by Allyn & Bacon
A Viacom Company
160 Gould Street
Needham Heights, MA 02194

Internet: www.abacon.com
America Online: keyword: College Online

All rights reserved. No part of the material protected by this copyright notice may be reproduced or utilized in any form or by any means, electronic or mechanical, including photocopying, recording, or by any information storage and retrieval system, without written permission from the copyright holder.

Previous edition published by Macmillan Publishing Company, copyright © 1994.

**Library of Congress Cataloging-in-Publication Data**

Root, Robert L.
    Wordsmithery : a guide to working at writing / Robert L. Root, Jr.
—2nd ed.
      p.   cm.
    Includes bibliographical references and index.
    ISBN 0-205-27024-7 (alk. paper)
    1. English language—Rhetoric.  2. Report writing.  I. Title.
PE1408.R668   1998
808'.042—dc21
                                        97-29543
                                          CIP

Printed in the United States of America

10  9  8  7  6  5  4  3  2  1    01  00  99  98  97

Credits appear on p. 151, which constitutes an extension of the copyright page.

*Still for Sue,*
*With gratitude*
*for shared grace*

# Contents

## *Chapter*  **6**

### *Going Public* *116*

*A guide to text preparation and packaging, readying a revised draft for another reader.*

## *Chapter* **7**

### *Wordsmiths at Work* *129*

*A review of the strategies of wordsmithery through writing samples from work in various stages of progress.*

# Preface

A preface traditionally is the part of the book that comes before the text and gives the author an opportunity to prepare the reader for what follows. This preface is addressed to the writer rather than to the reader because, whether you start this book thinking of yourself as experienced or inexperienced at writing, you should think of yourself as a writer while you read it. Reading like a writer will connect you more readily to the ideas and strategies presented here and help you become more open to the suggestions that you can apply to your own writing—the processes you take it through, the attitudes you bring to it, the aspirations you have for it.

*Wordsmithery* is a book of explanation and advice for the writer. It explains what practiced writers go through to successfully complete composing tasks they give themselves or are given by others; it shares their writing about writing; it provides alternative strategies used by experienced writers that will help inexperienced writers gain the success and confidence they need to develop as writers. The book is not strictly for a course in composition (although an *Instructor's Manual* is available with suggestions for ways to use it in a composition course); there are no exercises, activities, or assignments. Nonetheless, because I believe that the same strategies that make practiced writers successful will make successful novice writers mature, the book can serve as a companion to coursework, no matter what the course. More importantly, it provides a resource beyond coursework for those who can benefit from a little talk with other writers.

Chapter 1 is an overview of what writers have to say not only about composing a text but also about being a wordsmith—a shaper of language, a "forger" of texts; it discusses the ways master wordsmiths work at writing and what novices need to learn to work at it. Chapters 2 through 6 focus separately on the elements of wordsmithery: the uses of writing as engagement with ideas and experience before a text is intended; the preliminaries that help prepare the writer to engage in creating a text; the strategies by which a text can be created; the strategies to revise that text and carry it beyond its original draft; the ways to prepare a text to go public, out into the world beyond the writer's notepad or desk. Chapter 7 returns to the experience of writers by illustrating all the elements of wordsmithery in the work of individual writers; it is the practical counterbalance to the theoretical opening chapter.

A word of caution, which will echo throughout the book: The order of Chapters 2 through 6 should not suggest that composing can be reduced to self-contained units to be arranged in an inflexible sequence. Instead, the chapter order reflects the relative sequence in which these elements usually take place and the kinds of things that happen at the center of these activities with plenty of overlap and spillage with the surrounding elements and plenty of fuzziness about just where one ends and another begins. Although the book may be read in any fashion it pleases the reader— the individual chapters are designed to be consulted and serve as resources independent of one another—the brevity of the book has been deliberate, an attempt to get all the elements of wordsmithery together in a space where they can be encountered in all their interrelatedness, as un-self-contained and nonsequential as they occur in writing itself. Read the first chapter to get the general idea of what happens in writing and what writers need to know; read the middle chapters to see how to put the processes of writing into motion; read the last chapter to see how other writers have gotten through composing. Then put the book aside and write, consulting it for a hint or a strategy of wordsmithery you may need.

By writing *Wordsmithery* I have been able to able to put in one place everything I have to say about writing to people who want to write. I can't begin to trace how I managed to arrive in a place where I had anything at all to say about writing—the trail is too winding and, by now, overgrown—but I can at least acknowledge some influences: Carl Klaus, Paul Diehl, and Richard Lloyd-Jones at the University of Iowa; John Dinan and Susan Tchudi at Central Michigan University; Michael Steinberg at the Traverse Bay Teaching Workshop; conversations with working wordsmiths David Denby, Neal Gabler, Walter Kerr, Connie Leas, Susan Nykamp, Noel Perrin, Richard Reeves, Kathleen Stocking, and Tom Wicker; and the composing processes of Theresa Barber, Mari L. Guizzetti, Scott Lundeen, Mary Elizabeth Pope, Heather Powser, Brian T. Rees, Melody K. Sagorski, and Stacey E. Wargelin. I have been the beneficiary of Barbara Heinssen's intelligence, understanding, and patience; Katherine Evancie's keen eye; the recommendations of the reviewers of the first edition of the book; and the recommendations of the reviewers of the second edition: Richard P. Batteiger,

Oklahoma State University; Drew Colenbrander, Delta College; and Patti-Anne Hanlon, University of Nevada. Finally, I am continually encouraged by the emergent wordsmithery and mere presence on the planet of Becky, Tom, and Caroline and the support of my wife, Sue, in all things, including a writing life.

R. L. R., Jr.

*Wordsmithery*

# 1

# Wordsmithery: An Introduction

What I did not realize was that the constant honing of my perceptions and writing ability, the continual practice in trying to express myself, was laying the background for eventual acceptance in a field I had not even begun to explore.

—Sigurd Olson

**Wordsmith,** the descriptive metaphor for "writer" defined in the *Random House Dictionary of the English Language* simply as "an expert in the use of words," was a term only vaguely familiar to me, one I had never given much thought. Then, many years ago, Canadian teachers Lorri Neilsen and Christine Mowat told me they had become writing consultants or "career writers" and named their business Wordsmiths, Inc. Their job was to help forge the raw language materials of the workplace into something durable and serviceable. The term has stuck in my mind ever since.

Wordsmithery seems an apt term to me because it connects the writer's work to that of the smith—the blacksmith so capable of forming fundamental, functional products; the silversmith, so adept at fashioning both items for daily use and items of elegance and beauty that distinctions between craft and art became uncertain; the goldsmith, designing delicate ornaments from precious metal. All of them adjusted the shape of their materials and selected their resources to meet the demands of the task as well as the needs and interests of their clientele. Wordsmithery also seems appropriate as a metaphor for the writer because the smith's trade was learned through apprenticeship, trial and error under the supervision of an accomplished artisan, a master in both the sense of supervisor and the sense of teacher. *The American Heritage Dictionary* describes a smith as "one who works metal when it is hot and malleable." The apprentice wordsmith, then, may be imagined as someone sweating over paper-and-ink forges with hot and malleable ideas and words, now fashioning something durable and functional, now designing something delicate and ornamental, all the while striving for accomplishment in the craft of wordsmithery.

## The Making of a Wordsmith: Sigurd Olson on Learning to Write

As a writer myself and as someone who has interviewed and analyzed the composing processes of essayists, critics, and business writers, I am always looking for clues about the real world of writing—about the ways wordsmiths make themselves. Once, reading *Songs of the North,* a collection of writings by popular outdoors author Sigurd Olson, I was struck by his description of how he became a writer. Olson came to writing fairly late. He had grown up with a love for the outdoors, trained as a biologist, worked as a wilderness guide, and taught at Ely Junior College in Minnesota. Having read widely in nature writing himself, he eventually felt the need to communicate something about the natural world and his understanding of it through his own writing, and made the transition from teacher-outdoorsman to nature writer.

Sigurd Olson's account of his development as a writer reveals some crucial elements of writing in the real world. For example, Olson's very motivation for becoming a writer arose from his desire to communicate with others about specific subjects; his need to share his experience of the natural world generated his growth as a writer. Describing his years of development, Olson recalled "the gradual growth of facility through endless practice, day after day, the interminable disappointments, and the many false starts" (98). Wordsmiths don't do it right the first time, and they don't achieve their peak levels of performance overnight. Without the possibility of trial and error, it is arguable whether Olson would have ever developed into the writer he became.

The practice Olson mentions consisted of not only genuine attempts to write articles but also daily notes and observations.

Olson used writing both to learn writing itself and also to learn nature; his writing consisted at first of

> taking notes in the field on what I saw and thought about, descriptions of animals, birds, and the countless things observed on each foray into the wilds; until now I had always relied on memory. This was a new activity, and while at first my scribblings were almost incoherent, in time they became more meaningful; but far more important than the actual wrestling with the mechanics of words and sentences was that the very act of recording made me see things more accurately. The longer I tried to recapture scenes and events, the more I saw. (98)

"The very act of recording made me see things more accurately"—for the wordsmith, writing is a mode of learning as well as a mode of communicating, and this use of writing pushed Olson beyond superficial levels of knowing. Eventually, he tells us,

> There were times . . . when words and ideas came without effort, and I was conscious of something going on in my mind I had not felt before. Golden moments, because they were rare, it was as though writing generated an energy that tapped new sources of knowledge and awareness. (98)

At such moments in Olson's writing, his language did not simply represent reality as he already understood it, but rather served as a means of coming to know a reality. As composition scholar Kenneth Dowst has observed, "Language in a sense comes between the writer's self and objective reality. . . . [W]e do not know the world immediately; rather we *compose* our knowledge by composing language" (68–70). Through his writing Olson discovered what his understanding of the natural world consisted of. Even if he had never gone public with any of his writing, the private writing that he did for himself would have benefited him by expanding his comprehension of the world he lived and worked in.

Moreover, the writing, by preparing the way for his understanding, also prepared the way for his eventual publishing. As he observes,

> What I did not realize was that the constant honing of my perceptions and writing ability, the continual practice in trying to express myself, was laying the background for eventual acceptance in a field I had not even begun to explore. (103)

Ultimately, his dissatisfaction with the kind of work he had been producing led him to expand earlier ideas into the essays that became *The Singing Wilderness,* the book that established his place among nature writers, and he discovered "what I had always wanted to say" (107).

Olson's work in progress helped to generate further development both in writing and in understanding. The most deeply held beliefs often of necessity cannot lie easily accessible on the surface; to truly understand them and to discover the language to express them they must be mined, pursued laboriously beneath the surface. Writing not only expresses meaning—it uncovers it.

Furthermore, note that Olson discovered what *he* wanted to say—not what someone else wanted him to say. His great success as a writer ultimately came from that moment when, whether he satisfied a broader audience or not, he was achieving his own goals.

## The First Element of Wordsmithery: Personal Commitment

Sigurd Olson's description of his development as a writer echoes descriptions by other writers and in some ways encapsulates the elements of wordsmithery. To begin with, *an essential element of composition for wordsmiths is the personal commitment to their writing.* Time and again working writers have said that they write to please themselves first of all. By that, they do not mean that they are indifferent to demands made on them by potential readers or by specific occasions for writing. They mean that they need to accomplish their own goals for a project before worrying whether they have accomplished someone else's. Writers without goals of their own often fail to achieve those set for them by others.

Nancy Sommers, a researcher and teacher, has stressed the importance of students coming "to know what writers know," which is "how to bring their life and their writing together" (30). Bringing life and writing together generates personal commitment to writing. But personal commitment does not mean that these writers generate only personal writing, writing about their private lives and experiences. Instead, personal commitment opens the door to understanding whatever subject matter the writer chooses to engage with. It also helps generate the energy that carries the writer through to a satisfying and successful final draft. As journalist John Jerome writes, boredom "comes from trying to write things that offer no gear teeth for my interest. The most difficult work I know is to write about subjects one is not interested in" (95).

Sue Lorch, an academic writer, has described well the dilemma of writing about something without personal commitment. She tells how, as a college student, she wrote a "one-draft, sure-fire A paper" describing a painting in the college museum and was shocked to receive a failing grade on it. As she struggled unsuccessfully to revise it in hopes of a higher grade, she made a discovery about her own involvement with the assignment and the reasons her writing had bored her teacher:

> Not for life, love, or sacred honor (a concept intimately tied in my mind with the need to make As) could I conceive of the means whereby I could make my description more interesting. The painting wasn't interesting; it was, after all, of a bunch of cows standing in a nondescript field, and images of pastoral perfection and bucolic bliss did not accord with my view of the world in 1968. As the pile of yellow paper grew deeper, my mood grew darker. I was going to have to take myself to see that so-called art again, through the rain this time, and I didn't want to. I was bored into a near coma by the thing the first time I saw it, and the second time could only be. . . . Whoa. Wait. What had I just said? Had something of *me* inadvertently crept into a paper about a picture? Now I was in deep trouble. Not only did I have to go look at it, I was going to have to become interested in it. (168–169)

In the end she must return to the museum and get interested in the painting—commit herself to active involvement with it—before she can begin to write about it in any meaningful (and academically rewarding) way. Her experience is a common one in college writing, although not all students are lucky enough to get the chance to do the paper over.

Moreover, personal commitment is also important for the development of a wordsmith's voice. Much writing for academic courses is hampered by the writer's attempt to imitate the voices of established writers in the field, to sound like the authors of researched articles and textbooks. A good deal of academic plagiarism among students arises from an inability to present researched information in any other voice—or in any other words—than that of the original author. Worse, perhaps, a lack of personal commitment often prevents students from finding their own voice as solidly in their academic writing as in their personal writing. Even though the voice itself may be an academic voice, a professional voice, a scientific voice, or a conversational voice, even though it may shift to meet the goals of the writing task and the needs of the writing audience, if it doesn't reflect a personal commitment to the subject matter and the writing task, it will be an artificial voice, an unconvincing voice for the reader, an unsatisfying voice for the writer.

# T he Second Element of Wordsmithery: Immersion in Context

Sigurd Olson's remarks also illustrate *a second element of word-smithery, immersion in context*. Olson had a subject matter in which he was deeply engaged—as a student he studied biology out of personal interest; as a guide he studied the wilderness out of both curiosity and necessity. His growth did not occur devoid of context. In the same way, business journalist Susan Nykamp, formerly an excellent writer as a college student, had problems at the sentence level as a beginning staff writer for the Photo Marketing Association until she learned the photo retailing business thoroughly. Although she had been an outstanding writer in both English and journalism courses at her university, sometimes in her early experience as a practicing career writer her lack of background made it difficult for her to take phrases in her notes and work them into complete sentences—she simply didn't know enough about the subject to have options about what to say about it. But constant immersion in her field through conversations with colleagues, reading of professional materials, and continual writing made her sufficiently assured of her subject matter to be able to use her writing skills. Her rise to managing editor of a major publication, *Photo Marketing*, followed the arc of her growth in understanding of her field.

As researchers in composition and cognition have been telling us, writers cannot consciously juggle all the constraints of writing simultaneously. According to Carl Bereiter, for example, writers need to attend to written language production, controlled association of ideas, rules of style and mechanics, considerations of audience, aesthetic or critical judgment, and reflective thinking all at the same time. But these six skills are sufficiently demanding that consciously concentrating on one distracts from concentrating on others. As an extreme example, someone engaged in calligraphy, the art of graceful penmanship, has to have decided previously what will be written and cannot decide on language while concentrating on forming letters; any diversion of concentration toward meaning distracts concentration from letter formation.

To a lesser extent, all writers face these kinds of constraints. The only way that all of these skills can be competently expressed is if some skills become automatic, so that attention may be focused on fewer constraints at a time. Drafting a story, we worry little about penmanship, knowing we can concentrate on it in a later draft, or we ignore spelling and correct forms, knowing we can look them up later; preparing a final draft to submit to an editor, an employer, or a teacher, we concentrate on legibility, neatness, and correctness, and have difficulty attending to the sense. Similarly some knowledge of subject matter, writing strategies, and sense of audience need to be stored in long-term memory so that short-term memory can deal with limited constraints. It is this immersion in context that stores knowledge of subject matter; philosopher Michael Polanyi calls it the "dwelling in" a particular activity that leads to personal knowledge. As Sigurd Olson and Susan Nykamp show, in the real world, writing comes from a knowledge base that is neither arbitrary nor transient. In Thoreau's words, "How vain it is to sit down to write when you have not stood up to live."

Where writing arises out of a personal commitment and immersion in context, wordsmiths continually draw upon their background. The knowledge they have of their subject matter makes it easier for them to imagine writing projects they might successfully work on and gives them easier access to pertinent information when they need it. Both their learning and their composing are part of the same continual cognitive process. Composition needs a long gestation period, one that begins even before the writer is conscious of being pregnant with intention.

## T he Third Element of Wordsmithery: *Assiduous String-Saving*

Connected to immersion in context is *a third element of wordsmithery, constant involvement with an area of interest through writing,* what political columnist Tom Wicker has referred to as "assiduous string-saving," a tendency to take note of—and notes on—a range of subjects almost continually. Sigurd Olson models that for us in his copious fieldnotes; columnist Jim Fitzgerald of the *Detroit Free Press* stores items and comments about them in a continually growing and ever-changing folder. Columnist and teacher Donald Murray advises:

> Keep a planning notebook with you to play in at the office, at home, in the car, on the airplane, . . . while you're watching television, sitting in a parking lot or eating a lonely lunch. . . . [M]ake lists, notes, diagrams, collect quotes and citations, paste in key articles and references, sketch outlines, draft titles, leads, endings, key paragraphs. ("One" 148)

The late naturalist Edwin Way Teale, another notetaker, not only regularly took field notes but at the end of each day typed them up and dated, titled, and numbered them. Composition scholar Louise Wetherbee Phelps, keeping track of her writing over a three-month period one summer, found she "talked with family and friends, wrote letters, journals, notes, abstracts, outlines, essays, kept a reading journal, filled three daybooks with notes on my composing, elaborated all these in further notes, annotations and commentary, sketches and maps, drafts, on the computer screen" (245).

Henry David Thoreau, himself an assiduous string-saver, kept so thorough a journal that many critics have pronounced it his greatest work. Certainly it was the source of his major works. Often the journal entries served as Thoreau's zero or rough draft; we can trace specific passages out of *Walden, A Week on the Concord and Merrimack Rivers,* and *The Maine Woods* directly to daily journal entries. His journal was the source of inspiration and expression, the place where he could generate, incubate, and explore essential ideas of those later works. British novelist Virginia Woolf wrote twenty-six volumes of her diary between 1915 and 1941; Da Vinci, Darwin, Marx, Wittgenstein, Tolstoy, Freud, Emerson, writers and thinkers in every field, have similarly used diaries, notebooks, journals, and logs, and given voice to their most profound insights in the pages of their workaday writing before producing the influential and enduring works by which they are best known.

# T he Fourth Element of Wordsmithery: Discovery through Writing

Such interaction with the materials of one's writing is an important occasion for *a fourth element of wordsmithery, the discovery of ideas through writing.* The testimony that writing facilitates discovery has come to us from a multitude of sources, both literary and expository, in the real world of writing. Ideas tend to be vague and unformed until they are put into language, and the groping after language helps writers figure out what they want to say—what they want to mean. Critic Alfred Kazin once observed that "in a very real sense the writer writes in order to teach himself, to understand himself, to satisfy himself" (Murray, *Shoptalk* 38). The poet C. Day Lewis confirmed that impression when he insisted of his own writing

> I do not sit down at my desk to put into verse something that is already clear in my mind. If it were clear in my mind, I should have no incentive or need to write about it. . . . We do not write in order to be understood, we write in order to understand. (Murray, *Shoptalk* 106)

Journals and daybooks are places to discover and rehearse before attempting to draft and revise writing that eventually will go public. Writers in business and the professions find that not only notes but also drafts of memos and other informal communications are occasions for discovery. In college courses the writing up of notes and commentary on research help, writers to discover what they don't know (or else, in Robert Frost's phrase, to remember "something I didn't know I knew" [Murray, *Shoptalk* 101]) and prepare them for the later writing they must do to demonstrate their knowledge. Whether in preliminary workaday writing or early drafts, wordsmiths make a place for regular discovery through writing.

## T he Fifth Element of Wordsmithery: Understanding Composing Processes

*A fifth element of wordsmithery is a realistic understanding of the composing process.* Wordsmiths have customary work habits, practical expectations about the quality of early drafts, and confidence in their own ability to bring a "professional" text out of a formless mass of materials. Edwin Way Teale expressed this realistic understanding in a letter to fellow naturalist Ann Zwinger:

> I think the reason we dread the first draft of a book so much is not only that it is a time of endless decisions—what to put in, what to leave out, how to begin, how to end, etc., etc.—but it is the time when the book

we dreamed of writing, the book that has been floating in the air, so to speak, has to be confined by words on paper. Immediately there are intimations that the book is beginning to be less than we hoped it would be. The reason revision is so much fun is that little by little, day after day, we feel we are lifting the book back nearer the original goal. (Zwinger and Teale xviii)

The discouragement that comes with the first struggle with a draft is familiar to all writers of books, articles, stories, poems, plays, academic papers, research papers, essay examinations, convention addresses, formal reports, instruction manuals; the assurance that revision will banish that discouragement is something only writers who understand the composing process and who have successfully gotten through it can feel.

Having that confidence does not necessarily make the writing easier. As Teale says of his revision process:

These are my "Earthworm Days" when I am plowing back and forth through the paragraphs, loosening up lumpy or soggy sentences and enriching the book by inserting new facts and ideas as the earthworm enriches the soil by pulling pieces of leaves underground. Or, to put it another way, I am occupied these days folding over my manuscript in the sense that Thoreau meant when he wrote to Ralph Waldo Emerson: "In writing conversation should be folded over many times thick." (Zwinger and Teale xviii)

Experienced wordsmiths know that writing is hard work, but unlike the apprentice they know the rewards that lie beyond the labor.

Poet, novelist, and critic Elizabeth Hardwick, while claiming not to understand why the writing process works as it does, nonetheless has described how it works: "The brain slowly begins to function in a different way, to make mysterious connections. Say, it is Monday, and you write a very bad draft, but if you keep on trying, on Friday, words, phrases, appear almost unexpectedly. I don't know why you can't do it on Monday, or why I can't" (Plimpton 111). She observes of inexperienced writers that they often are overly disappointed by their first drafts: "They don't understand that they have merely begun, and that they may be merely beginning even in the second or third draft" (111).

Wordsmiths also have routines that help them write. Political journalist Richard Reeves, for example, will start writing at five or five-thirty in the morning and work productively before the outside world can interrupt him. He knows that his peak period of energy is early in the day, and he uses that period for the work he values most (Root, *Working* 119). In fact, so many writers work on that kind of schedule that when novelist Kurt Vonnegut attended an Eastern-bloc writers conference, almost the first question he was asked by one of the participants was: "Mr. Vonnegut, what do you do in the afternoons?" (Root, *Working* 122–123).

These writers also know that the writing isn't likely to be completed at a single sitting. When Richard Reeves attempted to write pieces nonstop, he could trace the decline of his energy through the pages of work; now he routinely breaks down longer tasks into manageable parts. Many writers have spoken of working regularly in short intervals over a period of time rather than trying to complete a project in marathon composing sessions. They settle for ten, five, even two or three pages a day, knowing that a substantial work will arise gradually. A student writing only one page for each class day in a typical semester would produce seventy-five pages by the end of the term or over one hundred pages if she also wrote one page a day on weekends, the equivalent of ten to fifteen class papers; at a rate of two or three pages a day she would double or triple the equivalent number of papers.

Many writers have testified to the same experience and routinely break down the composing of longer works into short sections or chunks. In addition to recognizing that revision will pull these sections together, they also know that, in fact, the work benefits from this piecemeal approach by extending the time to incubate ideas and to work subconsciously on writing. As Hemingway did, they often leave the work at a point where they know they can begin again the next day. Such a policy is an antidote to writer's block.

Studies of experienced and novice writers have demonstrated that the strategies for writing that wordsmiths draw on extend to the slightest, most reflexive actions. For example, when experienced writers pause in their drafting, they tend to reread what they have written and let the rereading help generate the next section of prose; inexperienced writers are apt to use those pauses to look out the window or up at the ceiling, as if hoping to find the next section floating in the air. The experienced wordsmith knows that the text she produces can help her continue to produce text; the inexperienced writer thinks the text merely records ideas generated or discovered in an outside world and cannot use the text to help him write.

# C omparing Experienced Wordsmiths and Beginning Writers: Some Advice

The testimony of accomplished wordsmiths supports the view that (to paraphrase William Hazlitt): "The more a person writes, the more a person can write." Clearly, the novice in writing can learn a great deal by serving an apprenticeship with such experienced wordsmiths, even if it is only conducted through the pages of a book like this. Moreover, beginning writers can gain by recognizing the elements of wordsmithery and the ways in which their own approaches to writing make it difficult to take advantage of those elements. The contrast between experienced wordsmiths and beginning writers suggests some obvious advice:

- For wordsmiths writing arises out of personal commitment, but for novices writing too often arises out of impersonal assignment and they act in response to tasks imposed on them by others, without a sense of investment or ownership in the writing project. Many problems in student writing arise not from lack of ability or potential but rather from feeling indifferent, apathetic, disinterested; looking for short-cuts to avoid spending time or energy; and making only a perfunctory, uncommitted effort. Advice to writers: Find a level of personal commitment that allows you to engage yourself in any writing project you face, even ones not of your choosing.

- Wordsmiths live immersed in a context from which they draw inspiration, incentive, ideas and information, and a knowledge of audience and writing plans, but novice writers may be strangers to the context of their writing, lacking knowledge of subject, format, style, strategies, or audience, perhaps lacking interest of their own. Advice to writers: Acquire context in any subject you write about (especially those where your initial knowledge is minimal) not only prior to writing but during writing as well.

- Wordsmiths draw upon the assiduous string-saving that makes their experience with the subject virtually an on-going act of prewriting essential not only for the individual product but for the act of dwelling in the context itself; novices, however, have no stored energy source on which to draw and often engage in jump-start writing, a spark from an outside power source necessary even to get their engines to idle because they have no self-starting ignition. Advice to writers: Become string-savers both in the context of short-term situations (such as a course in which papers might be assigned) and also in the context of long-term situations (such as a career that may frequently ask you to write about your area of expertise).

- Wordsmiths depend upon discovery through writing, whether in the workaday writing that constitutes a means of keeping abreast of their own thinking or in the drafting of communicative texts, but novices too often confuse writer-based prose (writing for themselves) with reader-based prose (writing for an audience), continually aiming for one-draft writing they hope to perform at a single sitting. Advice to writers: Allow yourself opportunities to discover through writing.

- Wordsmiths understand their own writing processes and draw on a range of strategies to focus their attention on what is most important at each moment of each process, but the novice too often assumes that the process is the same for all writers and attempts to follow a prescribed set of activities focused on the final product; by believing that such elements as written language production, controlled association of ideas, rules of usage and mechanics, needs of the reader, critical and aesthetic judgment, and reflective thinking can all be given equal and simultaneous attention, the novice virtually guarantees ineffectiveness at all of them. Advice to writers: Understand the nature of composing, including how others write as well as how you yourself write, so that you can take advantage of its elements and avoid writing episodes in which several constraints are operating simultaneously.

It seems to me that these elements hold true for writing across the board, whether in creative writing, academic writing, or professional writing. The student writer in a composition class is a novice in the same way that a beginner at creative writing might be, and success at writing for both of them may depend on adapting the techniques of the accomplished wordsmith. Regardless of whether the course demands attention to personal subjects and such forms as the essay and the memoir or focuses on academic subjects and such forms as the research paper and the critical analysis, student writers need to have strategies that let them

- engage the topic on their own terms as well as on terms of the assignment,
- discover what they know and need to know about the subject of the assignment and the form of writing it will have to be presented in,
- produce a draft of the text and work with it until it expresses the appropriate meaning in the appropriate form, and
- prepare it to go public in a presentation text that will not confuse or distract its reader(s) from its meaning.

The student accountant, political scientist, pyschologist, physical therapist, geologist all share these strategies in common with the critic, the technical writer, the business writer, the columnist, the essayist, and the poet.

Although we will continue to draw from the experience and advice of both accomplished and emerging wordsmiths throughout the chapters that follow, no attempt will be made to turn readers into committed artists; wordsmithery is about art for only a few practitioners—for the rest of us it is a necessary skill in the work we do, one of the daily accomplishments expected of us in our careers. Composition scholars Barbara Couture and Jone Rymer have made the distinction between two types of writers in the professions: "career writers," those hired for their writing abilities to accomplish specialized writing tasks in the industry, and "professionals who write," those hired for their abilities and expertise in particular disciplines and workplace roles who, nonetheless, are also expected to write frequently as part of their jobs. In the information age in which we live, most professional people will be "professionals who write," and an excellent way to prepare for that stage of a career is to learn effective strategies for composing in the precareer stage that college education provides. The following pages will offer specific suggestions for apprentice wordsmiths, whatever the orientation they bring to their study, in the hope not so much of their achieving mastery by the end of one slim volume but rather of their inculcating habits of working at writing that will set them on the path to wordsmithery.

# 2

# *String-Saving*

*It saves and makes available all those years of reading. Otherwise I'd forget everything, and life wouldn't accumulate, but merely pass.*

—Annie Dillard

For the wordsmith in any field, the generation of ideas for writing and the accumulation of knowledge in a topic most often grow out of what Tom Wicker has termed "assiduous string-saving," the constant collection of bits and pieces of information and ideas on a regular basis. String-saving can take any number of forms and is an element in the development of any writer in any field. The most famous example, perhaps, is that of Henry David Thoreau's journal, a work of forty-seven volumes kept over a twenty-four-year period. In it, he recorded and responded to his reading and his experiences, developed drafts of works he later published, and stored field notes on his daily observations. Tracing its progress from his youth to his death, we find in it the full range of his interests as well as evidence of the ways journal keeping aided in the development of his ideas.

Similarly, the string-saving of other writers in other fields has been an important part of their work. Charles Darwin's notebooks on the voyage of the *Beagle,* in which he recorded observations of plant and animal life, scientific speculations, and encounters with South American cultures, served as the basis for his later writing on the origin of species; Leonardo da Vinci's notebooks touch on a wide range of subjects, from scientific and philosophical to artistic and literary to personal, and contain drafts of letters, diagrams, sketches, treatises, fables, and jokes. Published texts are available of journals, diaries, and notebooks for a wide range of individuals, including politicians such as George Washington and John Adams, philosophers such as Søren Kierkegaard and Ludwig Wittgenstein, artists Paul Klee and Edgar Degas, dancers Martha Graham and Vaslav Nijinsky, actors David Garrick and Fanny Kemble, psychoanalysts Sigmund Freud and Karen Horney, composers Tchaikovsky and Poulenc, inventor Thomas Edison, religious leaders John Wesley and Brigham Young, naturalists Audubon, Burroughs, and Muir, poets Sylvia Plath and May Sarton, novelists, dramatists, essayists, explorers, revolutionaries—the list is long and varied.

## S *tring-Savers at Work*

The point, of course, is that these works were not simply compilations of daily trivia, such as meals eaten, hours spent awake, persons met in conversation, although that may be a portion or the whole of some diaries and journals. Rather they were places in which the authors could speculate on the conduct of their own lives and the process of their own thinking, record seemingly random bits of information for further reference, and try out the expression of ideas in a context free of the pressure to prepare a polished text. Virginia Woolf believed that keeping her diary made it easier to do her other writing: essays, reviews, novels. She wrote that

> the habit of writing thus for my own eye only is good practice. It loosens the ligaments. Never mind the misses and stumbles. Going at such a pace as I do I must make the most direct and instant shots at my object, and thus have to lay hands on words, choose them and shoot them with no more pause than is needed to put my pen in the ink. I believe that during the past year I can trace some increase of ease in my professional writing which I attribute to my casual half hours after tea. (13)

The "increase of ease in professional writing" that grows out of daily "casual" writing occurs for most writers who do it. Without some sort of string-saving a writer can approach a writing project unprepared both in an understanding of the topic and in a familiarity with the kind of language appropriate to the project. This often happens to writers in the workplace and routinely happens to college writers, particularly freshmen and sophomores taking courses in a wide range of disciplines.

Thoreau was aware of the importance of string-saving as an long-term activity. He once flatly stated, "A journal is a record of experiences and growth, not a preserve of things well done or said" (Dillman 15). The growth comes from making connections that only come about through writing:

> Having by chance recorded a few disconnected thoughts and then brought them into juxtaposition, they suggested a whole new field in which it was possible to labor and to think. Thought begat thought. (Dillman 14–15)

As Thoreau describes it the value of the journal is twofold: first, to record thoughts, observations, and experiences independent of all other entries, and second, to discover further ideas by noticing and creating connections among the individual entries. In essence, Thoreau is endorsing the view that both comprehension and learning involve connecting new information to knowledge a person already has. Writing is a highly effective way of making those connections.

The travel writer Tobias Schneebaum reinforces this view in an account of his own journal keeping. While living among primitive tribes in the jungles of Indonesia, Schneebaum used his journal extensively, as so many travel writers do. He writes,

> My journal was always with me, and I wrote up the day's events as quickly as possible, knowing that even the most important happenings can easily be forgotten. The journal calmed me and forced me to think clearly about the day. Often the day had been muddled with so many things happening one after another that the only way to straighten it out was to write about it, reliving it until the pattern of incidents sorted itself out. Recording specific information had to be done as soon as it was learned. . . . (148–149)

Careful and thorough journal keeping not only recorded specific information but helped Schneebaum to understand it and, later, to connect it to other information he was recording.

Annie Dillard, a poet and essayist, began to keep a journal after college, "finding myself highly trained for taking notes" ("How" 20). In over thirty journal volumes, "all indexed," compiled since she began her journal keeping, she keeps "mostly information in the form of notes on my reading, and to a lesser extent, notes on things I'd seen and heard during the day."

> If I want to write about Arctic exploration, say, or star chemistry, or monasticism, I can find masses of pertinent data under that topic. And if I browse I can often find images from other fields that may fit into what I'm writing, if only as metaphor or simile. It's terrific having all

these materials handy. It saves and makes available all those years of reading. Otherwise I'd forget everything, and life wouldn't accumulate, but merely pass. (20)

It may be that journals and notebooks record ideas and resources where the writer can retrieve them, but it may also be that the act of recording ideas, experiences, and resources helps the writer retain them better within herself.

## **T** *he Purposes of String-Saving: Recording, Responding, Rehearsing*

As these various writers suggest, the use of string-saving varies with the writer and the writing project. Some writers who draw on their own experiences and observations out in the world use string-saving methods to record and react to whatever they encounter firsthand; other writers who draw on the data collected by others use string-saving methods to record and react to whatever they read; some writers do both. Working on an essay about a trip to Mesa Verde, I found myself consulting my journal entries on our travels, brochures and tourbooks we'd picked up along the way, and articles giving me historical background that I located once I decided to write on that topic. Working on an academic article about a teaching controversy, I read widely in what others had written and published about the subject, took copious notes and quotes from them, and consulted my string-saving as I planned my own article. In the first case the casual string-saving I turned to was there because I had kept a journal routinely, with no intention of producing an essay; having written about it in the first place was one of the factors that helped me decide to write about it in a form that could go public and gave me the resources to do the job. In the second case, while I had some background knowledge to begin with, I didn't have enough to write an academic article with and had to do a lot of research and specific task-centered string-saving. In either case the string-saving helped me better understand what I was writing about.

Journals, notebooks, and diaries are not the only means of string-saving. String-saving is a flexible concept that changes shape with the individual—some write things down on file cards and file them meticulously, others jot things on scraps of paper and stick them places haphazardly, still others store items in folders and scrapbooks, and others may use a combination of these. On a European trip Ralph Waldo Emerson kept one overall journal, separate journals for each country, and a pocket diary for memoranda. College teacher and academic writer Mary Croft has called herself "a file junkie" who saves "ideas, quotations, anecdotes, techniques, suggestions, notes from conference presentations . . . adding to my storehouse keeps me alert, growing, learning" (43–44). The individual writer has to find the method that works best for him. Researchers suggest that various techniques work best for various purposes—for example, to accumulate a broad but superficial knowledge of a topic, note taking is useful, but to gain a narrower but deeper knowledge, journal keeping is more productive. Writers rarely do only one or the other.

The apprentice wordsmith, then, can draw on the experience of the journeymen wordsmiths—if experienced writers engage in assiduous string-saving as a routine part of their approach to writing, then inexperienced writers ought to consider ways of string-saving themselves. String-saving serves three purposes: recording, responding, and rehearsing.

- As a means of *recording,* it preserves resources the writer may want to have available in the future and helps to gather the topic knowledge necessary so a writer can begin to write.

- As a means of *responding,* string-saving provides a chance for reflexive interaction with ideas and information; the mere act of recording demands some effort at interpreting and drawing conclusions, but it also invites further reactions and discussions in writing that help the writer to understand the subject and to stake out her own position about it.

- As a means of *rehearsing,* string-saving can serve as a way to practice manipulation of language, ideas, and forms of expression prior to an occasion where actual drafting might begin; such rehearsal frees up the writer's concentration at the time of drafting so that it can be focused on such items as structure and organization or development of portions of the text.

Regular occasions of writing for yourself make eventual writing for others easier in the same way that regular occasions of exercise make strenuous physical activity easier when necessary—you don't prepare for the Boston Marathon by watching a lot of television, at least not if you have any hopes of completing the course at all; the same may be said for writing.

## F orms of String-Saving

Wordsmiths use a variety of forms of string-saving, depending on the kinds of writing they do or the approaches that seem to work best for a specific project or personality. Among the most productive are journals; logs; dialectical notebooks; abstracts, summaries and précis; annotations and marginalia; notes; and commonplace books, folders, clipbooks, and scrapbooks. Most writers use more than one means of string-saving.

### Journals

Journals are made up of frequent entries that explore ideas, record observations, detail experiences, and react to events. People who keep journals often use them to write about the entire range of their experience, but often journals are focused on specific topics or events, such as a travel journal, a subject-matter journal, or a project journal. Some writers keep more than one going at the same time—they might keep a personal journal for reflecting on daily activities and observations, as a place to think by writing, and also keep a response journal for both recording information from their reading and reacting, as a place to store material to be consulted later. Mary Elizabeth Pope, then a graduate student, once explained,

> I keep several journals—one personal and one academic/professional. I can't just sit down with an assignment and say, "Okay, how will I do this?" For me I have to sort of "brew" the idea for a while—make notes on paper or a tape recorder, explore ideas—at first, a lot of this is random—while I'm eating breakfast, or in the shower, or having a conversation with someone. Also, *talking* about the idea also leads me into the things I am usually struggling with. I *have* to write these *all* down, otherwise I lose them.

In addition to recording ideas and observations, the act of writing pushes her to respond to her topic. Many writers find that writing tends to set thought in motion, even when they think they have no thoughts about a topic. Writing usually activates the writer's engagement with the subject under consideration and generates deeper reflection than do more passive approaches to thinking. The mere attempt to put into words what the writer doesn't understand about the subject or the reading usually leads her to the point where she discovers that she does have something to say about the topic. She cannot remain aloof or uninvolved. This approach is so often effective that some students keep a journal for each course they are taking; others use one journal for the semester but make daily entries cumulatively, writing a portion after each class session or composing a thorough rundown of the day's classes at the end of each class day.

Some writers keep a process journal in which they comment on the ideas, progress, and strategies they use for composing a work-in-progress; the process journal is a means of working through to an understanding of the writer's own work habits and composing knowledge. Even experienced wordsmiths find the process journal helpful. "At age fifty-seven I find myself still learning to work," John Jerome has written.

> Keeping a journal focused on writing matters has taught me more about how to work than anything else I've ever done. I can't say too emphatically how valuable it is to keep a journal, if for nothing else than as a way of examining one's own working methods, for finding out how you can be more productive—and therefore less frustrated. (245)

Some writers are reluctant to learn about their composing processes because they are afraid that, once they know what they're doing, they won't be able to do it. However, without that knowledge, it is difficult for them to realize which of the strategies they use are really counterproductive and need to be avoided. It is also difficult to be able to select more productive strategies. Process journals help you get out of your own way in your writing.

Journals usually differ from *diaries* in the sense that a diary is often intended to record the minutiae of daily life as a kind of on-going historical report about the author written a day at a time, but in practice the two forms often overlap. For the most part they should be spontaneous or impromptu. They should be not an attempt to write crafted, polished prose but rather an attempt to write informal, unmediated prose. Journal entries are most effective when the writer works at an entry long enough to develop ideas and push himself beyond preliminary generalizations. Very brief entries are fine for purposes of recording, but they often do not generate connections or allow room for new ideas to develop. I usually advise my students to write for at least twenty-five to thirty minutes, which produces entries two or three pages long; in my own journal keeping I may write for only a few minutes or for a couple of hours, depending on the time available and the subject of the entry.

I use journal entries for many purposes, sometimes to talk over problems I'm encountering in my work or in my personal life, sometimes to plan writing I hope to do, sometimes to think through my intentions and strategies in work-in-progress, sometimes just to record where I am and what I'm doing. The following journal entry was written July 23, 1979, at the end of the day at the house of friends in Grosse Pointe, Michigan, near Detroit, about a three-hour drive away from where I lived. I had picked up a hitchhiker on the way, and in this journal entry I was simply trying to record some of the things I had observed about her and some of the impressions she had made on me.

JOURNAL ENTRY

## July 23, 1979

I don't exactly know what made me stop to give her a ride. I don't usually pick up hitchhikers, male or female, partly because of the danger and partly because it's uncomfortable sitting with a stranger. Kathy was in blue jeans, sandals, and a white tee-shirt, her thumb out, a tan soft suitcase stuffed to the top by her feet. I pulled over and watched her run towards me in the rear-view mirror.

She opened the door and stuck in her head, her long red hair blowing across her freckled arms and face. She smiled and asked where I was heading. I explained I was only going as far as Detroit but that was okay and she got in.

I learned some things about her in the half-hour or so that she rode with me. She played jazz piano at the Oakland Center on Wednesday nights; taught or tutored students part-time, on a contract basis, for Oakland University's music department; was disappointed that her sax man's wife kept him from joining her for the weekend. She had hoped to get a job playing piano for the night somewhere. She had $2.35 with her. She had had good rides so far and just hoped no one hassled her, that she got in no hassle she couldn't easily get out of.

She was from Rose City, near Flint. When she saw the Renaissance Center in Detroit, it freaked her out, she said. She said she had to be back on Monday, that usually she was living with some dude and couldn't really have a vacation, that guys she knew went out west and had a good time with hundreds of friends.

When I told her I knew someone at Oakland but hadn't seen him for years she said I should just go sit in his class—it would freak him out.

We talked about vacations, how I hadn't done much. She encouraged me to just take off. She had never been to Canada, didn't know where she was going when she got there. I dropped her at a Total station near the tunnel to Canada, wondering if she would easily get across, wondering what would happen to her.

Most of this entry is information, record keeping, because the experience interested me and I wanted to remember it.

The next day when I woke up I realized that our conversation about vacations had struck a nerve in me, that the real reason I wanted to remember it had to do with a contrast I saw between her and me. I added to the journal:

## July 24, 1979

I wondered something else while talking to her. I wondered why I at 36 had to wait and worry about finances and all the things I had to get done before I could get away while she at 22 or so could dare the world, unknown, on $2.35. Was I so afraid of life I could not grip it without safety measures all around me?

Had I not tried to record my impressions of my hitchhiker, I might not have realized that it was not only her personality that had struck me but also what her approach to life revealed to me about my own approach to life. Often a journal entry doesn't merely record your experience but brings you further toward understanding it.

### Logs

Logs are made up of brief entries recording experiences, responses, and events. A log in nautical use records locations, experiences, and actions of a vessel, almost like a form of bookkeeping. But a log can also be a record of immediate reactions to circumstances and readings, such as a reading log, which accumulates the writer's reactions to assigned or self-chosen texts, or a student-teaching log, which records classroom observations and reactions. A writer might record a summary of information gleaned from a specific piece of reading and perhaps note connections with other readings, or he might record the work accomplished that day on a particular project and suggest what work will be done next. In a sense such logs record the progress of intellectual journeys.

Logs are often kept in diaries or record books with limited areas for entries. When I use logs in my courses, students use 5" × 8" note cards and take from three to ten minutes to complete them, with an injunction to be concrete as much as possible. In the following typical writing log entry, a student provides a summary of work-in-progress to record points raised about a draft discussed with other students and to remind herself of where she needs to go next with her revision.

## WRITING LOG

In order to revise my paper I will begin by examining the beginning and comparing it to the ending. Then I will have to ask myself whether it (the end) accomplishes my goal. So far, I do not think it quite does. I also need to add more detailed description of what that event in my hometown was like. It seems as though I get a little off the topic by the end of the paper. That, especially, needs to be taken care of.

In a reading log entry another student focuses on an essay she has read outside of class, "At the Buffalo Bill Museum" by Jane Tompkins, and reflects on her reaction to it in regard to her own writing.

## READING LOG

The introduction was good. It fed the reader with lots of specific information. This author uses excellent word choices. The words used were easy and descriptive. I liked the way the author displayed examples, events, sights, and exhibits throughout the essay. This helped me visualize what I was reading.

I have problems writing my papers and making sure I have good details! This essay helped me see where to put my details and how to know where to put them. The author in this essay also describes how she feels at times, like on page 222. I feel it's important for a reader to understand the author and her feelings. Like I previously stated, the best part of this essay is the language and the detail the author uses.

Log entries should be as long as they need to be to adequately discuss the information the writer is dealing with; in an independently kept, self-generated log, entries might vary greatly in length.

## Dialectical Notebooks

The dialectical notebook is a systematic exploration of the writer's thinking composed of double entries. The writer writes a journal entry on an assigned or self-chosen topic and then reacts to that entry by writing a second entry analyzing the first. Often this is done by making each entry only a page long and writing them on facing pages. Variations of this technique are called the double-entry notebook and the living journal. In essence this form is dialectical because it creates a give-and-take between two roles—a primary observer and a secondary analyst—played by the same person; it pushes the writer toward a deeper understanding of his response to a specific experience than a single entry would allow him.

Some writers find this approach particularly effective with coursework and research. The first page abstracts, summarizes, or records some aspect of reading the writer has done for the course or for the research project, and the second page analyzes the first page by trying to find another way of expressing its ideas, reacting to the information, connecting the information to other information already collected, or projecting the kind of information the writer still needs to collect in order to understand the subject fully. Particularly where the information is unfamiliar, this kind of approach allows string-savers the opportunity to wrestle with their understanding and expression of the material, to make it their own. This is especially important if, eventually, they are going to have to explain it in more formal writing to others.

Journals, logs, and dialectical notebooks all attempt to create conversations with the self; in the dialectical notebook the second entry extends the conversation from a monologue to a dialogue within the self. It is particularly useful as a way to push writers to analyze their reflections. Moreover, you need not keep a dialectical notebook per se in order to use the technique for analysis; any journal entry or log entry can trigger a follow-up response entry.

## Abstracts, Summaries, Précis

Abstracts, summaries, and précis are all condensations of specific texts. Writers use them to put ideas from someone else's texts into their own words or forms, in part to record them in a briefer, more accessible format, and in part to learn how to talk about them in terms familiar to the reader doing the abstracting. Particularly with complex, complicated, and unfamiliar ideas, wrestling with words and terms leads to better understanding. A good deal of learning on the job and in the classroom derives from conversations and attempts to manipulate concepts with others. Although abstracts, summaries, and précis can also be formal pieces of writing (abstracts in particular are used in many disciplines), employing them as informal pieces of writing serves the writer as a means of conversing with himself about these concepts. Such informal pieces of writing can also serve as journal entries or log entries, although they work well when written on note cards, so that they can be sorted out when needed.

## Annotations, Marginalia

In the course of reading other people's texts a reader might write comments in the margins or at the beginning or end of the piece, recording reactions, noting structure or lines of argument, making observations about ideas or language or connections to other texts, all of which could be consulted another time in order to jog the reader's memory or to provide a brief guide to the text. Especially in cases where the reader will have to return to the text as a source of analysis or commentary, such techniques give more power to the initial reading and help the reader to retain a sense of what has been read. They also enable the reader to interact with the text, helping her better understand both the reading and her own reaction. Ronald Primeau, in his book *Writing in the Margins: From Annotation to Critical Essay*, gives as an example poet–painter William Blake's annotations of artist Sir Joshua Reynolds's *Discourses*, a published series of lectures on art. Blake's annotation takes the form of a running commentary on Reynolds's discourses, at times agreeing or approving ("True!" "Excellent!" "Good advice!"), at times disagreeing or disapproving ("This is all false & self-contradictory." "Nonsense."), at times commenting and arguing ("Mechanical Excellence is the only Vehicle of Genius." "What is Laying up Materials but Copying?" "Why imitate them at all?") (58–64). By carrying out a one-sided conversation with Reynolds's book through recording his own reactions to its ideas and assertions in its margins, Blake is able to interact with his reading and develop his own ideas and assertions.

The importance of interacting with reading should be apparent. Writers often have difficulty writing about a text when they read it through and try to write about it from memory, without having annotated it or without having previously responded to it through some form of string-saving. Even dog-earring pages with information or ideas that catch your fancy as you read gives you a way of retrieving a book's highlights later on, a place to come back to when related ideas surface in other reading later on.

Writing in the margins helps not only in general reading but also in academic research. For example, as part of a project in one of my classes, students were asked to read three encyclopedia articles about armadillos and write up an article of their own based on the information in those sources. (They all read photocopies of the encyclopedia articles.) One student began by quickly reading all three articles through to get the feel of them, then reread each one more carefully, underlining the main idea in each paragraph and writing key terms in the margins so that later she could lay all three articles side by side and notice their similarities and differences by her marginal notes and her underlined or circled quotes. Another student took the approach of simply reading the first article very closely, numbering and labeling each new subtopic in the margin as he went down the page until he had completed the reading and made a thorough annotation of the article. Then he turned to the next article, reading closely again, using the numbers from the first article to note where familiar subtopics appeared, and giving new numbers and labels to new subtopics. He went on to the third article in the same way and then used his numbers and labels to compare data among all three articles. In either case the annotations in the margins helped record the different kinds of subtopics available and helped the writers get an overview of all the information scattered among the three articles. Both could refer back to their marginalia when they began to work on the writing project by organizing outlines to guide the drafting (as we'll see in Chapter 4).

## Notes, Field Notes, Lab Notes

Notes are the record of observations, to be consulted and analyzed later on. The travel writer Vivian Gornick, author of a book on Egypt, tells of "knowing each day I had to get it down, get it down, worry later about what it meant. And thank God I did. If it hadn't been for the extensiveness of those notes. . . ." (106). Making notes on the spot, instantaneously, is more likely to preserve information. Film reviewers and music, theater, and dance critics often keep notes during a viewing of a performance, sometimes writing their notes without looking at the notepad, a few to a page, covering many pages during a single event. The notes remind them of the aspects of the performance that caught their attention and help them relive the experience when they come to write about it.

In this electronic age we sometimes forget to engage information through writing because we do not always receive it that way. Studies of note taking in college show that students retain information longer and understand it more fully when they keep notes, but the culture we live in is so visual and aural that many students tend to simply "view" classes as if they were situation comedies, rather than interact with them through note taking. Television, radio, telephone answering machines, and tape recorders all transmit information orally and some even record it, but hearing and seeing does not preserve information as reliably as writing. By the same token photocopying preserves text but does not make any one read it. Writing notes not only gives writers something concrete to refer to but also forces them to become engaged with their information on some level. This is the standard way of preserving new knowledge in the classroom, but the writer too often associates it only with classroom learning instead of with outside learning as well.

Even more useful is the habit of returning to notes and elaborating on them. After Edwin Way Teale made field notes on his outdoor rambles, he came home, typed them up, and catalogued them, giving himself a chance not only to preserve them in a clearer form but also to review and perhaps revise them before he became too distant from the immediate experiences that created them. As with so many of these techniques, the act of recording and responding is as important as the actual preservation of the information. While it is often valuable to have notes to refer to, sometimes the mere writing of the information helps to preserve it in the writer's memory. Moreover, often the notes help trigger more detailed memories and reflection that the writer might have trouble recalling without some sort of written memory aide.

## Commonplace Books, Folders, Clipbooks, Scrapbooks

Some forms of notebooks are used chiefly as storage areas, not only of the writer's own ideas but also of the texts of others.

Traditionally a commonplace book was a place to copy significant or well-written passages from other works, perhaps for possible use in quotation later on but chiefly to record ideas of immediate interest regardless of any specific intentions for later use. The philosopher John Locke developed and published a systematic method of producing a commonplace book and indexing it in order to accumulate topics and information to be used in writing. They have been kept by people in many fields. Economist R. H. Tawney's commonplace book recorded comments, conversations, plans of possible books, and observations about political events. Novelist E. M. Forster's commonplace book included quotes from and comments on his reading as well as copies of his own letters. Thomas Jefferson began a literary commonplace book as a boy and kept it until he was thirty, recording passages in Greek, Latin, and English from a variety of poets, dramatists, and philosophers. A clipbook is a collection of clippings from newspapers and magazines; file folders and scrapbooks can be used as commonplace books and clipbooks. By the same token, those who keep journals often copy other texts into them. The string-saver saves not only her own thoughts but those of others as well, because writing doesn't take place in a vacuum—often it takes the discovery of a new piece of information or the encounter with someone else's point of view to trigger connections and start an avalanche of thought that sorts out or completes half-formed thoughts and ideas.

## A *pproaches to String-Saving*

In all of these examples the writer attempts to record and react in circumstances where he is not inhibited by the pressures involved in producing a formal text—worries about format, structure, unity, development, logic, style, or mechanics. These kinds of regular written engagement with ideas of interest to the writer help develop both the writer's understanding of the topic and also the writer's facility with language about the topic. The key elements of string-saving are *informality* and *regularity*. All writers, no matter how experienced, struggle most with their writing when they try to deal with topics about which they are unfamiliar, uncertain, or inexperienced and when they write only intermittently, spending long periods without writing anything. Much—perhaps most—school-based writing that is incoherent or illogical or banal comes about because student writers have not understood either the topic or their own expression of it. Like experienced writers wrestling with writing after a long layoff, student writers who only engage in writing infrequently during a semester, perhaps only when a major assignment is due, usually find writing more arduous and frustrating (and unsuccessful) than those who write regularly. For both the accomplished wordsmith and the novice, assiduous string-saving is a way to foster the constant engagement with ideas and language that leads to understanding and clear expression. String-saving immerses the writer in a context and leads to a better comprehension of the context—a possible end in itself; writing is more rewarding and somewhat less painful if it arises out of a context in which the writer has been immersed.

Clearly then the apprentice wordsmith ought to begin string-saving. Here are some recommended approaches:

- Set aside time at the beginning or the ending of the day to write for a while in a journal, giving yourself at least twenty to thirty minutes.

- Take time *during* important reading to make notes and time *after* reading to write a response, sitting down to read with an open notepad or a couple of file cards.

- Keep a log focused on a long-term project—a college course, a series of meetings, a number of field trips—in which you react in writing for four or five minutes at the end of each episode, as a way of summarizing the events and ideas.

- Take a few minutes *before* classes or meetings or trips to write about what has happened so far and what is coming up, getting yourself back into the context of the experience.

- Review and flesh out notes frequently, making certain that you understand what your own notes refer to and that you can write complete sentences about the ideas you record, perhaps even writing a brief summary of the notes.

- Set up a system of string-saving that seems appropriate to your specific projects and general interests as both a prospective writer and a thinking person. In college courses look for an approach that keeps you engaged with course content and class sessions and helps you record the ideas and rehearse the language of the course. In professional life look for an approach that keeps you acquiring background material, reflecting on your experience, and expressing the language of your field. In personal writing look for an approach that keeps you recording experience, responding to ideas and events, and rehearsing language in your own voice.

Writers with specific projects in mind should begin by using writing to think about the subject and record necessary information, but string-saving should also become a constant act of unspecified preparation for the life beyond the project. A journal or notebook or a daybook should be a constant companion; even bursts of writing at coffee breaks and unexpected occasions can eventually save a lot of string.

For the student writer this may mean knowing in advance what papers need to be written in a course and string-saving for those particular projects, but it also means string-saving for the long haul, for the career beyond the course, the courses beyond the assigned papers. A good many studies of the effects of journal keeping have demonstrated that they are long lasting and deep and pave the way for more expansive thinking and more thorough knowledge. Students who have routinely kept logs, journals, and notes in courses have demonstrated not only greater success with formal writing but greater overall performance in those courses. At the outset of the semester, at the beginning of each course, some plan for regular string-saving ought to be set in motion, regardless of whether the individual instructor assigns one or not. A few minutes a day of response to a class period, a few lines per each assigned reading, accumulate a wealth of resources over a semester.

**T**he Wordsmith on the Word Processor:

## String-Saving

Wordsmithery can be done almost anywhere. Logs, journals, poems, songs, stories, essays, and articles have been drafted on napkins, paper towels, toilet paper, and scrap paper with pencil, pen, crayon, eyebrow liner, and lipstick. Writing is a portable art, and those writers who prefer less haphazard means of composing routinely travel with journals and daybooks in their pockets and bookbags or with portable typewriters or with laptop computers, even computerized notebooks. Many writers still prefer to compose in longhand, in part because typing their compositions seems to give them a neatness and permanence that makes it harder to revise them, but also in part because the slower transmission of words from the brain through the hand to the paper through hand-writing allows for more changes, adjustments, and alternatives to be considered in the very act of drafting—the computer helps the writer transmit more words more quickly but doesn't auto-matically slow down their generation or allow time for automatic alteration.

Nonetheless the word processor has made much of the clerical, mechanical side of writing—the preparation of readable texts—faster, easier, and less frustrating. Anything that can be done in longhand can be done on the word processor, and the wordsmith ought to consider it not simply a glorified typewriter but a flexible instrument for strategies of wordsmithery. To further the develop-ment of wordsmithery on the word processor, we will set aside this space at the end of the central chapters of the book to suggest some specific strategies, such as these for string-saving, on the word processor.

**Journaling.**   I carry around a journal in my bookbag for personal reflection, a small notebook for recording information I stumble on, and a variety of colored pens. But I also keep a work-in-progress journal on the computer. This is the place to talk specifically about what I'm working on and how it's going. The nice thing about this journal is that I often use it to draft portions of work in progress while pretending only to be talking about what I would be doing if I were drafting it—like the unsent letter we'll talk about in a later chapter, journaling is a writer's way of tricking himself into writ-ing something at a moment when he feels incapable of writing or hemmed in by the restraints that sometimes accompany drafting. It's a way of getting out of your own way, and it works very well for me.

**Process Logs.**   One way to get a sense of accomplishment about a work-in-progress is to spend a few minutes before you quit for the day recording what you've done on a project and predicting what you'll do next when you return to it. This is a project file you can add to incrementally and use as a way to get yourself started each time you come back to the project. Sometimes work on a specific project is interrupted by work on other projects, and the writer has difficulty getting back in tune with that specific project or return-ing to a focused concentration on it. A process log can help you locate your position on the project and revive your concentration. Simply read over your log of work sessions and remind yourself what has been accomplished and where you need to go next.

Perhaps write for three minutes on what you will do that work session. Then you should be ready to approach the work-in-progress draft itself.

**Note Files.** The cut-and-paste, copy-and-paste, and duplication commands of most word-processing programs make it efficient and practical to keep files of notes and quotations from sources as you work on a project. In place of note cards you can simply build files on various topics and, where appropriate, copy portions of those files into later drafts of papers. If you copy accurately the first time—and I have often observed people sitting in libraries with laptop computers doing exactly that—you will not be recopying (and possibly making errors) but simply transferring the identical text. For example, I kept a computer file of quotes from writers I had run across since the first edition of this book, and when I began revising it, I referred to that file and transferred sections to insert in my text as I worked with it. Mary Beth Pope's remarks earlier in this chapter are examples of material stored in that file. Even if I had not used those quotes, my having copied them into the file in the first place would have helped me to remember them, to have gotten the ideas in them into my subconscious. As it is, the file not only serves as a resource for a project like this book but also preserves a compact record of those ideas on a topic of interest to me for future use.

**Source Files.** In addition to keeping a file of notes or quotes from references, on projects involving other sources I keep a running bibliography on file. This is a place to accurately record the references I have consulted on the project. Sometimes I annotate that bibliography with a few comments about what is in each source; other times the list simply contains references in the forms I might use on a works cited or bibliography page. Because I can copy and insert this in my paper, it is easier and more efficient to keep it separately, so I can be very thorough while I research and be very selective when I insert or delete items in the list of references I attach to my paper. Moreover, since my word-processing program has a hanging indentation command, I can easily format my bibliography in the style most manuals on research papers and articles require.

**Conversation.** Throughout the book I will advocate talking to others as a way of working at writing. Journaling, logging, and dialectical note keeping are simply ways of talking to yourself, getting a conversation going with only one participant, whereas conversation with others allows you to rehearse language and experiment with expression in a casual and unconstrained way. On the word processor this can happen with chat groups, where you can electronically eavesdrop on others' exchanges or contribute to them yourself. It can also happen simply through e-mail with friends, classmates, or colleagues. Several writers I know correspond with each other frequently by electronic mail, as a middle ground between actual conversation and mail correspondence. E-mail has the advantage of being quick; chat groups can happen in real time just like conversations, but because you have to type your contributions, you and your correspondents have the opportunity to revise them and be a little more specific about what you communicate. Trying out ideas for papers or passages that might go in papers by sending them on e-mail to another reader who shares your interests, background, or assignment is a good way to think through information and narratives. For some of my correspondents, just as sometimes happens in conversation, the very act of expressing themselves about a topic is sufficient to help them reach a new level of understanding about it, whether I respond or not. And the same happens with me—trying to find the words to explain something I know or something I think to another person helps me better understand what I know or what I think. In my e-mail program I can also preserve the messages I send as well as the messages I receive, and I can print them all out if I need a hardcopy file for reference. (I often need to read print copy rather than text on the computer screen.)

# 3

# *Starting*

*Somehow this is necessary to generate the idea—to truly find my direction, even though I may have thought I knew what I was doing and where I was going ahead of time. I need to internalize ideas before I can externalize them.*

—Mary Croft

String-saving is a way to be constantly immersed in the context of your daily thoughts, readings, and experiences. It keeps you thinking, analyzing, synthesizing, connecting; as a string-saver you are involved in the subject of your string-saving, extending your knowledge, changing its shape. Its primary value for anyone is its ability to promote greater learning and deeper understanding of a topic, a field, or a discipline, and in this regard, even if it led no further, would be worth doing for its own sake.

But string-saving also creates a reservoir of ideas and topic-specific knowledge to draw upon when you decide to write. For people who are continuously or repeatedly involved in writing, any writing is a preparation for future writing, even if they have no particular projects in mind when they make entries in journals or record something on note cards or in commonplace books. The same activities that help you learn the subject help you prepare to write about it. Because writing is a means of discovery as well as a means of communication, sometimes the wordsmith discovers a topic or a project through the act of string-saving; projects grow out of connections made on the pages of a journal or ideas juxtaposed in a daybook. At other times a project arises from a request from others to present information or analysis—a memo explaining your position on a subject to a committee on which you serve, a formal report to a board of directors, an assignment in a course you are taking all arise as requests (or demands) from others. In either case, no matter how projects arise, the wordsmith often goes back into earlier string-saving as a way to get material and look for connections to aid in an understanding of what is being proposed.

Moreover, composing possibilities can also be explored and advanced through further informal writing used to discover, gather information, generate ideas, speculate, or plan. Such preliminary activities sometimes take place without writing when the topic is the focus of intense mental activity, not only consciously but also subconsciously—perhaps even unconsciously—but most writers are aided in the drafting of a composition by first having written their way through phases of preparation and initiation, no matter how vague or rough that preliminary (*pre*) writing may be.

## T *he Preliminaries of a Writing Project: One Example*

Any one of a thousand ideas bubbling under the surface of your consciousness, simmering in your memory, percolating in your string-saving could eventually erupt into a writing project, but whether self-generated or instigated by others, a writing project usually needs some sort of stimulus to set it in motion. For example, on one occasion my department chairperson was hosting a meeting with English department chairs from other colleges and universities. He needed some sort of culminating event to follow a dinner meeting; it had to be informative or thought provoking and involve their professional concerns but also entertaining and enjoyable, since the group would need a break from the intense discussions they had had all day. He asked me to consider doing some sort of presentation on media and to let him know if I could come up with something.

Realizing I had some time to consider what to do and whether I should do it, I pushed it to the back of my mind. Sometimes the ideas in the back of my mind get lost because they don't find anything else to connect with back there and because more urgent ideas—ones I can see connections for—demand more attention and jostle them to the shadows and sidelines. But as it happened with this suggestion, there was a lot back there to connect to—as my chairperson knows, I've written a book and several articles about popular media and taught several different courses in it over the years. Moreover, one aspect of media had been the subject of conversation among my fellow teachers and me in recent months because of a concern for visual literacy on the part of agencies accrediting teacher education programs in English.

One morning after breakfast, while taking a shower, I started to think up a presentation on visual literacy to present to the other department chairs, all of whom would have to wrestle with the issue in their curricula. I remembered some scenes from films based on literature that I use to make my students "visually literate" in a literature and film course I regularly teach, and I then remembered some commercials I had shown in a guest lecture for a friend's class in broadcasting. I thought of a title, thought of how much I could present in a thirty- to forty-minute period, thought of the main points I would be trying to make and how those film clips and commercials would illustrate it. After showering and dressing, I went to the computer and typed up a journal entry explaining to myself what I had been thinking about, saved it, and then revised the journal entry into a memo to my department chair, suggesting what I would like to do and inviting his reaction.

Essentially then, I was accepting an assignment to write a lecture about media and checking in with the person who had given the assignment to see if I could take my own approach to it, which would be more rewarding for me, and also to see if my approach met his requirements, which would be more satisfying for him and his audience. The initial impulse does not have to come from me but before I can do it, I need to understand whom I would be addressing, what the occasion for the address would be, what circumstances of presentation length and delivery style I would need to keep in my mind—that is, I need to understand the rhetorical situation that is prompting the project. I also need to know what it would take to do it successfully—what information and examples I already have, what ones I would need to acquire, what possible arrangement of information and examples I might pursue, perhaps what I know for certain and what I need to discover. In this case I know I have a pretty good general idea, some very good specific examples, and only a vague idea of what conclusion I might reach after presenting this information. That is enough to get me started; I know there is a writing project here worth following through on.

## W hy Preliminaries Matter

Very few writers are adept at finding a topic, generating and gathering information, organizing the content, planning the potential structure, and predrafting a piece of writing entirely in their heads. When the writing appears to come out spontaneously, as it sometimes seems to for some writers, it is usually a result of constant immersion in the topic and long familiarity with the genre or format. Columnists and critics may be dealing with new information or a new focus for their reflections in their columns and reviews, but they do not have to discover simultaneously how to write columns and reviews; business writers may consult new data when they write memos or reports, but they do not also have to research the forms in which they are writing or approach the subject matter as completely unfamiliar material; academic writers usually write up their analyses and conclusions drawn from new data or new perspectives, but they use forms familiar to them from previous papers on similar topics for similar occasions and audiences. In all these cases, familiarity with the kind of writing they want to produce, in terms both of the typical language they use to talk about the subject and also of the sort of structure they might use, allows them the freedom to focus on ideas. Moreover, familiarity with the subject allows them to focus on specific ideas about which they have certain knowledge rather than expend their energy discovering whether they know enough to write on a certain topic. These are the advantages journeyman wordsmiths have over apprentices, the kind that come with experience and repetition of similar writing tasks.

Preliminaries are important in composing because they can ease the difficulty inherent in almost any writing project and determine its degree of success. To draw on the metaphor of the writer as wordsmith, preliminaries involve gathering the materials, creating the design to be followed, and discovering goals specific to the project as well as general to all smithery. A smith must know before he sets out the nature of the metal he will be working with, the expectations of the person for whom the artifact will be fashioned, the condition of his forge, his bellows, his molds, his tools; he must have some knowledge of the design he hopes to follow, the various stages he will need to go through to transform raw material into carefully shaped, crafted, and polished work. Accomplished smithery is not a matter of simply pouring your own molten materials into some universal standard mold prepared by someone else but of creating your own mold to accomplish your own design; it is not firing up a forge and melting lumps of base metal in hopes of coming up with something as you go along and cutting down the work time by eliminating preparation. In all forms of smithery, including wordsmithery, avoiding preliminaries only makes the work harder, not easier. To come to the actual drafting well prepared, the wordsmith needs to remember a few essential tenets and choose among a range of strategies.

## The First Tenet of Preparation: Know Your Reader and Your Requirements

*The first tenet is to know who your reader will be and what constraints or requirements you will be under in the final draft you produce.* If a writer is writing for herself, she can let the format and the sense of the reader be ruled by her own inclinations and instincts, essentially guided by her own taste; but if she intends to submit her work to a publisher, an editor, a committee of her peers, an employer or supervisor, or a teacher, she would do well to consider what demands of length, format, and design will be made and who the audience will be for the piece she is writing. Some academic writing, for example, is fairly rigid as to structure and design, perhaps requiring discreet sections such as an introduction, description of research design, discussion of results, and conclusion; certain forms of documentation must be used, following specific style sheets and professional manuals such as those prescribed by the Modern Language Association (MLA), American Psychological Association (APA), or other disciplinary groups; certain principles of argumentation and presentation must be adhered to and others avoided. Most writing is done within a generic range—that is, if someone elects to write science fiction, there are limitations on what he can do before the work is no longer science fiction; if someone elects to write for a periodical focusing on theoretical research, there are limitations on what ideas for practical application he will be allowed to present.

Similarly, in classroom situations the nature of the assignment determines the kind and quality of prewriting and drafting that needs to be done. The teacher usually has something specific in mind for the assignment, something she hopes you will learn, some skill you will demonstrate, some knowledge you will display. The topic of the paper has to be related to the topic of the course, the degree to which the paper depends on individual analysis or researched synthesis of others' ideas is likely to be specified in the assignment and there are usually implicit, sometimes explicit, limits on the range of topics and approaches you can take to the assignment. Understanding that a teacher assigning a research paper in a college chemistry class is unlikely to accept unresearched personal reminiscences as fulfilling the assignment is essential information; knowing limitations of length, format, and design helps define the task to be accomplished in the paper.

The information on constraints imposed on the writing task is available in the assignment sheet, the memo requesting the report, the call for manuscripts, or consultation with the teacher, supervisor, coworker, or editor. In most cases you can find out what kinds of writing have been done by others along the lines you intend. Teachers often make sample papers available for study so that students can see what has been done for certain assignments in the past; handbooks and style manuals often reprint successful research papers; editors and publishers encourage writers to read their periodicals before submitting their writing, because a familiarity with what has been published gives the potential writer a sense of whether he wants to attempt that form and what is really being asked of him. By the same token, it is a standard observation that a writer should be a reader of the form in which he intends to write. If you have never really read a movie review, you have little likelihood of producing one; if you have never read an academic paper in your discipline, you have no sense of how to produce one.

Moreover, if you only ever produce one example of a specific form of writing, you have little possibility of growing as a writer in that form—and that goes for academic research papers as well as sonnets. Some of the difficulties writers face in academic fields are not only understanding specialized subject matter but also—and at the same time—learning to use the language of the field, write in the voice of its practitioners, and use the formats and genres of specialized texts. Familiarity with the forms you will be writing in and the audiences those forms are directed at makes some of the constraints you face in your writing less constraining.

## The Second Tenet: Schedule Sufficient Lead Time

*A second tenet is to give yourself plenty of lead time on a writing project.* Never try to do things in a hurry with a piece of writing that matters. Overnight wonders only happen when a writer has incubated and planned and rehearsed a piece of writing for a considerable period beforehand; attempts at fast and furious first-and-final drafts usually give themselves away by their incoherence, shallowness, and disunity. Setting a train of thought in motion allows a long period in which it can gain momentum; things happen subconsciously to the work when it is allowed a period of gestation. In classroom writing it is always good to know as soon as possible what the major writing assignment will be, not because you can get it out of the way sooner—usually an assignment due late in a course has been scheduled for that time to give you a chance to benefit from reading assignments and class discussion before writing—but because an awareness of a task ahead of you gives your subconscious an opportunity to work on the planning and the gathering of materials and, eventually, on the rehearsal of the language you propose to write.

In addition to granting yourself sufficient lead time, it helps to develop a time frame or tentative schedule in which to get the writing done. That means breaking down the parts of the project and the stages of the process and scheduling deadlines for accomplishing things. Projects involving research generally take longer than projects drawing on reflection, simply because research usually means examining far more material than the final work will use directly and also because merely accessing data from other sources than your own memory and experience is more time-consuming. Developing a time frame also means scheduling periods when you can do the work, particularly if you are not a full-time writer and other aspects of your life intrude on your writing time (demands of your job, your homelife, your other courses). Imagining a concrete schedule helps you decide how much lead time to give yourself. The less certainty you have about what you are going to do and how you are going to do it, the more useful it is to build in time for running up blind alleys and putting yourself in the way of unexpected discoveries. Even when you are confident and secure about your writing plans, it is wise to give yourself more lead time than you might predict you need—often our achievements don't conform to our intentions.

A rudimentary composing schedule would allow

- time for preliminaries, whatever they may be;
- time for drafting, including additional time for taking care of problems you could not have predicted that the drafting itself reveals to you;
- time for revising the piece once you are able to see it as a whole (and in spite of the revising you might have done during the drafting); and
- time for preparing the final copy of the text to go public.

These are not discreet stages—some portion of any of these activities occurs during most of the others—but trying to attend simultaneously to all of them (and to all of their subactivities as well) simply guarantees giving none of them the attention they need to be successfully, thoroughly completed. Even a relatively short-term project can be scheduled for lead time: If a professor wants an assignment two days from the class in which he announces it, you can still plan and ponder the assignment in a journal entry after class, start a draft that night or the next morning, revise it and prepare the presentation text the second night, and turn it in on time. In the interval between the preliminary writing and the drafting, you will be able to gestate much of what goes into that draft.

## The Third Tenet: Write before Drafting

*A third tenet is to try to do some preliminary writing before starting to work on an actual draft.* All writers use some sort of prewriting to prepare for drafting, whether in string-saving or in particular acts of prewriting; the kind of prewriting you do will depend on the circumstances of your composing. Someone who writes the same kind of piece, of the same length, for the same audience, in the same tone, such as a columnist, may find it necessary only to jot down a few notes or a vague, cursory outline, or to go through an intense period of contemplation; someone who is working in a new form for a new audience on a new subject in unfamiliar circumstances ought to do a great deal of preliminary consideration. In either case prewriting will help make more certain the likelihood that the initial drafting session will be a productive one. People who launch into writing without prewriting generally are at the mercy of their stream of consciousness—whatever connections they uncover or invent as they write determines the direction of their writing, not a bad procedure for a preliminary act of discovery but usually a disastrous one for any attempt at a formal draft.

Having said all of this, I need to add a caution. Just as it can be frustrating to try to write without having done any preliminary work, so it can be counterproductive to think of preliminaries as something that have to be accomplished totally before drafting can begin. Being overprepared is often as troubling as being underprepared—*the real goal of preliminaries is to get you prepared sufficiently to work well once you begin.* Sometimes the trick is knowing when to stop preparing and start drafting. Gathering materials together and planning the work to be done should give you confidence that the project can be completed, but no amount of preliminary work can cover every contingency that will emerge in the writing. Writers need to leave room for discovery and learning to take place not only before they begin composing but also while they are drafting and revising; moreover, they need to trust in their ability to adjust to discoveries whenever they occur.

## S *trategies for Getting Started*

A variety of strategies is available for getting started. The following alternatives do not exhaust the possible approaches nor should they be seen as mutually exclusive. Some strategies work better for certain kinds of writing than for others or serve as only one of a number of approaches that a specific project may demand.

### String-Saving Review

String-saving often serves, intentionally or unintentionally, as the preliminary writing for specific writing projects. Travel writer and explorer Mary Kingsley, for example, drew upon not only her notes and diaries but also upon her letters to friends and family for the voluminous information she acquired during the exploring that led to *Travels in West Africa*. Speaking of his first book, another travel writer, Tobias Schneebaum, claimed, "Without my journal to read, without the letters I wrote to friends at the time, I couldn't have done any factual writing" (163). His second book turned out to be a disappointment for him because he had no journals,

> nothing to work from but my memory and a few letters that friends had returned. . . . For me the book was a disaster. . . . [I]f I had worked from a journal I might have turned it into something more cohesive, more interesting. At least I would have had a perspective on the writing. (164)

Whether or not you intend your string-saving to be a form of prewriting, when you turn to the development of a subject on which you have written in journal or notes, you often find that a considerable amount of the preliminary work has been done, almost unintentionally, and the subsequent planning and preparing comes more readily.

## Rehearsing

Rehearsing is a form of unwritten composition, working ideas in language in your head. It is the imagining of the words you hope to say to start the first conversation with someone you are attracted to, the words you think you will need to say to make your case in a predictable argument, the words you wish you had said during an awkward social situation. Anne-Marie Oomen, in an article titled "Talking to Yourself in the Car is Okay," reminds us that we all "talk to ourselves," whether silently or out loud.

> You get into a conflict with someone but find yourself so dumb-founded by this person's stupidity, rudeness, arrogance, or bullhead-edness that you can only stutter your defense. You leave the scene wordless, looking like a great wimp. Twenty minutes later the conversation replays in your head and suddenly the most brilliant responses come to you. Your words are sharp and clever and you are so articulate that you could negotiate the Middle East peace talks. You offer stunning quips, dignified argument, rational logic, and absolutely cow your conversational opponent. (174)

Everyone rehearses language all the time, not only after events occur but also in anticipation of them. Experienced wordsmiths realize that rehearsal can be an aid to writing throughout the composing process, in preliminary work, in drafting, in revising.

Mostly this takes the form of writing in one's head while doing something else. Academic writer Mary Croft describes the experience well.

> For shorter pieces I begin by allowing ideas to roil and roll around in my head, usually as I am driving and preferably traveling over familiar roads—like the seven miles between home and the university. This can go on for some time. I try ideas out, looking at them from many angles. I phrase them, rephrase them, discard them, replace them—all the time "hearing" myself talking aloud in my head. I allow them to play around until the ideas catch and flow, until they have satisfied the inner critic (at least temporarily). Somehow this is necessary to generate the idea—to truly find my direction, even though I may have thought I knew what I was doing and where I was going ahead of time. I need to internalize ideas before I can externalize them. (41–42)

The rehearsal experience—"internalizing ideas before externalizing them"—prepares the way for later rounds of composing; it primes the pump, as it were, so that words flow more easily when the wordsmith sits down to write.

The interior monologue, however formless and spontaneous it might be, can be directed, nudged toward the writing project. Before I spend twenty-five minutes exercising on our cross-country ski machine, I read through notes or journal entries or drafts of work in progress so that I can begin rehearsing my planning, drafting, or revising while I exercise, staring out the window or at the curtains. Then the interior monologue will continue in the shower or on the drive to work, and when I sit down to write I find I have a lot to say—some writing gets done every time. Writers who don't know about rehearsing are apt to come to a composing session unprepared, unprimed. They often sit in front of the typewriter or word processor or hunch over the notepad, waiting for something to happen and growing more anxious about not writing (and making it harder to write by the minute). Journalist John Jerome takes a daily walk for rehearsal time, using it "to get immediately away from work, forgetting about it for ten minutes or so, then letting it roil back up to the surface of the mind. The result, usually, is new insights, new ideas, clearer phrasings. Sometimes I think I use walking as a way of getting away from the writing machine so I can think" (203).

## Listing

A simple and direct way to start is to make lists. For example, for an essay about growing up in your hometown, you might list five or six memorable experiences you had, moments that involved you and other people in your community. Or if you know generally an incident you intend to write on, you might list events in the order they happened or list people involved and what each of them was doing. If you are uncertain about the direction you need to go, you might list a series of tasks you need to perform to get the information you need or resolve the uncertainty you feel about the project. The point is to give yourself something to work with. Former drama critic Walter Kerr would start work on a review by transcribing and cataloging notes he had written down in the theater as he watched a performance. Copying the notes over into a more legible form and grouping them under various headings gave him a way of figuring out what he was interested in during the play and, to some extent, it also placed him back in the experience (see Figure 3.1). The groupings he discovered by doing this helped him figure out the items of information that were most important, both for learning what he thought and also for planning the order in which he wrote about things (Root, *Working* 138–162).

GEN —So hard to react. Surprised an empty living r

—lot of light considering only 2 oil lamps in place ([?])—
R bring 1 later—

—[?]

—Ghosts grown lightweight in my lifetime—

—'I learn of my story'      O to Liv

—AUD laugh O's description [?]

—incurable syph, incest, blackmail (refrain form calling BI
arson, but I think Ibsen burned that place down)—

—Light lavender wallpaper, furn not as overstuffed as usual—

—L was in dining room 'laying out some silverware' when heard
husband + housemaid (1st Ghost report      O + R)

—'Social convention! Do you know I think that's behind all the
<u>mischief</u> in world today!'      L

—'What about the truth?'      L
'What about ideals?'—JN

LIGHT —'Well we're all descended from such a union' she a coward, not
true      O sister R—L

—LV 'All ghosts, our mothers + fathers live on inside of us'      L

LANG —'lots of celebrating, lots intoxicating beverages passing around'      Eng

—'the more returned, the less'—

—'How dare you set yourself against your father?'      JN to R

—'Oh, that was when I was a little tie-over'      Eng L

—W + H      'O is upstairs resting—<u>on a sofa</u>?'      L

—O 'Mother my spirit has been broken, ruined!'

—O 'Regina is my one hope of salvation!'

—LV 'Because I'm going to tell them everything' TWICE! before
interruption, FINE 2nd. AUD laughs CA's–if it wasn't,
it should have!

**FIGURE 3.1** *Listing*

## Cataloging and Segmenting

Another way to get at the material you have or to organize it as you acquire it is to catalog it. John Jerome gets himself going by writing in a journal he keeps on the word processor; he calls it "an electronic notebook," "a rolling memo," "a kind of scratch pad for the day's work." After fifteen minutes or so

> I go through and, using the organizing power of electronic writing, flip the appropriate items into their own files. Moving the various ideas into new places serves a double purpose, because every time I move something out of the journal I review it, rethink where I might possibly use it, and, usually, polish it slightly; I see ways of touching it up, of changing the emphasis or reorganizing it for clarity. I begin to get a new look at what's underneath it. (161–162)

Working on a long magazine article about New Hampshire, he created five electronic files, typing up his notes as he gathered them, then moving them to files on a recent trip, personal memories, New Hampshire history and folklore, physical geography, and the ongoing draft as it develops (51–52). The cataloging helps him organize and review his material; it also helps him put off considering some material until he needs it, allowing him to work on smaller segments.

Segmenting a project gives the writer something more manageable to work with than the entire piece—a section, a chapter, a scene, a paragraph. As Richard Reeves once put it, describing the creation of a documentary film script, "I can't write a script. No one can write a script. But I can write a scene, and if I write enough scenes, eventually I've finished a script." Thinking about the parts you might productively work on, rather than thinking about the whole, gives you some chance to make progress on a writing project and gives the more uncertain segments the opportunity to develop from the discoveries you make in drafting. For longer pieces Mary Croft uses the interior monologue "to discover direction" but then works "in segments, not necessarily in the order in which they will eventually appear," working "from files of material on each segment" (43). In the earlier example of the visual literacy presentation, I might choose to work on the scenes from literature segment or the rhetoric of commercials segment before worrying about the conclusion or the beginning, expecting the completed segments to help me understand what goes into the uncompleted segments and trusting in the revising process to overcome difficulties of overall organization, transitions between segments, and coherence throughout.

## Clustering

Clustering is a technique in which you write down a word or phrase in the center of a page, draw a circle around it, and then move outward from it by recording a random series of words and phrases related to it, letting yourself connect things as you think of them. The point is not to organize orderly and attractive clusters but to get as much down on paper as quickly as you can, letting ideas simply come as they come, attaching them to the main circle or to subclusters where appropriate but focusing more on the volume of ideas than the structure. In a sense the network of clusters lays your knowledge of the topic out in front of you and lets you make choices about what to focus on, decide what additional information you need to get, and choose what knowledge you have that you can ignore. You are creating something to work with, possibly discovering that only one subcluster makes a worthwhile focus for your paper and feeling free to throw things out rather than force them into your writing plans. The essay, article, or paper that grows out of this approach might focus on a single dense grouping or several branches that seem related in significant ways, whereas branches that seem to trigger few subclusters might safely be ignored. (See Figure 3.2 for an example of clustering someone might generate for an essay on growing up; subsets such as those around "the house we lived in" or "adventures" or "Willow Park" actually served as the bases for three different essays.)

## Diagrams, Maps, Tables, Graphs, Flow Charts, Grids

One way to work with ideas is to find a way to represent them visually. The visual representation can serve as a way to remember the relationships among the parts, but the process of fashioning the image also helps to sort out its relationships. For example, a student assigned to read Mary Shelley's *Frankenstein* might notice that the novel begins with a few chapters written by an ice-bound explorer named Walton, then changes to a story narrated by Victor Frankenstein, that in turn contains a story narrated by the creature Frankenstein had brought to life; the student might then notice that Frankenstein's narrative continues after the creature's ends and that Walton's continues after the death of Frankenstein to the end of the book. Other features of the novel might also capture the student's notice, such as the isolation of the narrators, the theme of friendship and companionship, and the physical movement of the main characters. In attempting to sort out these

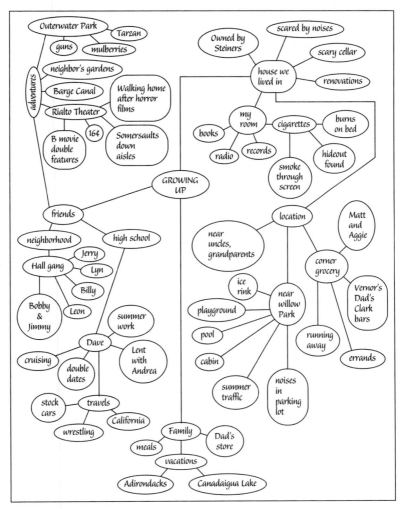

**FIGURE 3.2**  *Clustering*

elements the student might fashion a diagram (such as Figure 3.3) that helps clarify the relationships among characters, actions, and narratives in the novel. Such a diagram might help sort out the elements that need to be addressed in a critical analysis of the book and help determine which materials ought be included and which discarded in the draft to follow.

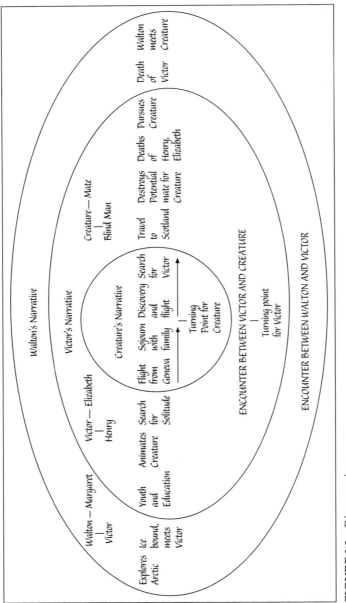

**FIGURE 3.3** *Diagramming*

Other forms of visual representation perform similar acts of sorting and arranging information, making relationships clearer, presenting a panoramic overview of the project, breaking information down into its component parts, and finding ways of arranging the information for purposes of examination. Mapmaking can stir memories of events in a particular place—my students use them to start papers on growing up in their hometowns and being in high school—or, more abstractly, show stages in a process or procedure. Tables work well to arrange numerical information and data that can be expressed in brief terms; graphs give visual representation of measures of change over time; flowcharts work best to represent sequences, processes, and hierarchies.

Information grids help organize any writing project based on close examination of a series of readings (such as a college research paper). The writer engaged in such a project could begin taking notes on the ideas and evidence one specific source deals with and comparing that with a second source and then a third and so on. To make the inquiry more methodical and systematic, she might create a grid composed of boxes in which specific items of information about the topic were placed. (See the example in Figure 3.4.) Across the top of the grid would be placed the names of the sources of this information, and down the left-hand side of the grid would be listed the categories of information those sources discuss. This approach helps the writer to identify what is important to a majority of sources and what is important to only a few; it also helps classify the types of information being gathered.

The point is to provide yourself with some means of investigating and examining information in writing and then to select and narrow the portions to be used in the paper or discover what gaps in knowledge need to be filled before writing. As forms of prewriting, all of these can be useful approaches to making sense of complicated material and giving the writer some way of arranging the parts of a project and preparing smaller units to work on rather than tackling the entire project at once, right from the beginning.

## Free Writing

Free writing works particularly well when you feel stuck because it gives you a way to be spontaneous about your preliminary writing. To free-write, you make yourself start writing and keep writing *nonstop* for a set period of time, usually ten minutes or so. You might

| Reviewer (Magazine) | Aeschliman (National Review) | Anonymous (Economist) | Brookhiser (Commentary) | Elson (Time) | Meilaender (Christian Century) | Riga (Choice) |
|---|---|---|---|---|---|---|
| Sense of Wilson's Purpose | demonstrate L's "profound effect on modern world" | wants to persuade intellectuals to reexamine Lewis | to show how Lewis speaks to present generation | to show how difficult consorts justified L's sainthood | to psychoanalyze Lewis | |
| General judgment | thorough, judicious, beautifully written | | shows signs of haste, too often chatty | | | clearly best bio; satisfactory despite flaws |
| Strengths of book | literary knowledge strong, literary argument convincing | | understands import of L's plumbing irrational depths of rel & childhood | | L's merits as lit critic, informative, witty narrative, lively, readable | |
| Weaknesses | limited philosophy knowledge, overest. L's signif., value | | emphasis of lit. crit of L. misplaced | | judgments puzzling; overinterprets; snide, condescends | speculations seem ill-advised or just wrong |
| Focus of review | emphasis is on Lewis as a philosopher | stresses L's rel. ideas, compares to Kipling | L. as Christian apologist; bio of a "public Christian" | focus on L's relationships w/ two difficult women | reliability of W's interpretations, tone, attitude | compare biographies of L; W's best but difficult |

FIGURE 3.4  *Gridding*

give yourself a phrase to start you off ("If I had to write an essay about my hometown I would write about . . .") and let yourself write whatever comes into your head for the next ten minutes. The initial sentences may read like gibberish ("If I had to write an essay about my hometown I would write about—who knows what? I certainly don't, because there's nothing I want to write about, particularly not in that town. After all, that's the place where my sister would have been voted Potato Queen if it hadn't been for . . .") but eventually you find yourself with something more substantive to write. The act of forcing yourself to write nonstop for a set amount of time "frees your writing" by keeping you from having to have something prepared before you write. As student writer Mary Elizabeth Pope has said of her course journals,

> I'd start responding to an article, for example, just because I had to— and then suddenly I would discover I had a very strong opinion about the topic and lots of things to say about it. It was really amazing and I have used it since to figure out problems I've had (especially writing papers) in other classes. If you are bored with a topic try to write about it. I've found that somehow you cannot remain uninvolved when you are freewriting on a topic, even if you initially had no interest in it.

Free writing helps you find out what is on your mind and avoid the internal censor or taskmaster who sometimes inhibits drafting by being too critical or too anxious about results too early in the writing. From the act of free writing you can discover a topic or a position or a difficulty that will initiate other acts of prewriting.

## Looping

The looping technique extends the experience of free writing by "looping" back to something in your initial writing to surface as the focus for the next round of free writing ("My sister being cheated out of the Potato Queen title really made us all angry with the community; I even did some vandalism to get even with them, because . . ."). Additional rounds, if necessary, continually start with some small part of the previous loop ("When I smashed the mayor's front window because my sister did not get the Potato Queen crown, it summed up my anger against the town . . ."). Many inexperienced writers start a piece of writing far too generally or broadly to sustain the draft they intend; the paper never really gets down to the "real" subject before the writer runs out of steam. Looping is one way of focusing before drafting.

## Conversation and Brainstorming

Talking things over with others gives you the advantages of other perspectives and the need to clarify what you mean. Conversation is often exploratory, people not so much explaining their positions as discovering them in the process of explaining them. A good listener who asks interested questions helps the speaker dig deeper. In the same way, a brainstorming session in which people bounce ideas off of one another has the advantage of sparking connections—someone else's idea reminds you of something you might not have recalled or helps you understand your attitudes better. Students trying to get a grasp on the requirements of an assignment can particularly benefit from brainstorming because it helps them discover a range of ideas they might not recognize on their own. Sometimes students can benefit from talking to their teachers, not so much because teachers can advise them about the potential of their work-in-progress (which they can) but more because the simple act of trying to put ideas into words helps clarify them. A good many writers have learned to interact with others as a way of working through plans and problems in their writing. Sometimes the interaction takes the form of writing groups, where people meet to discuss one another's work in progress, an idea that is often adopted in classrooms but too often avoided by students outside of the classroom; study groups meeting to discuss coursework might be even more productive if they were to discuss assignments-in-progress as well. But primarily what the writer needs is a sympathetic sounding board giving her the opportunity to work actively on her writing through language.

## Unsent Letters

Like journal entries, unsent letters are a way of discussing work-in-progress informally, and also like journal entries they help at any stage of writing. The idea is simply to start a letter to someone you know explaining what you're working on, what you hope to accomplish, and what problems you're having that you need to resolve. All of this helps to clarify the work-in-progress by giving you an informal occasion and a sympathetic reader and reducing the stress of producing something formally. In the end you don't bother to send the letter but use its insights in planning the draft of the work. Sometimes portions of the letter end up as portions of the work-in-progress.

### Zero or Discovery Drafts

Zero drafts are forms of the paper that are carried out before the rough draft or first draft—that is, before you are really making much of an attempt to take formal control of the paper; they are also called discovery drafts, because you write them simply to give yourself some sense of what you might say about the topic you have chosen (or had chosen for you—these prewriting techniques are particularly effective with academic assignments imposed on student writers). Even if you do not keep a journal or a dialectical notebook or the like, you can write a zero or discovery draft simply to find out what you know and how you might talk about it. The zero draft works most productively on writing projects that depend on your prior knowledge, material that can be drawn from experience or memory, because it helps discover problems of organization as well as usable material; it works less well with research writing projects because you may initially have less prior knowledge to discover or organize. In practice, a writer who starts a draft before he is really ready may end up producing a zero draft without intending to. The trick then is to recognize that this draft has simply provided a base from which to begin planning (and prewriting) ways of writing a new first draft that is more on track.

## S *tarting an Essay: One Example*

As a follow-up to these ideas, consider the following example of preliminary work on a writing project. A local newspaper had a Sunday column called "Our Place, and Yours," which was composed chiefly of pieces sent in by readers. In a class I was teaching I assigned my students to write for the column and helped prepare them by giving them reprints of several columns, reading and discussing them in class, and pointing out the requirement that the piece be no more than 450 words long. We considered the kinds of stories the paper was publishing, talked in small groups about ideas for the column, wrote journal entries about them, and shared drafts in class. I decided to write along with my students; in thinking about possible topics that would be appropriate for the column I remembered my reaction to the hitchhiker I had picked up four years earlier and went into my journal to find the entries about her (see Chapter 2). To get me started on the drafting I wrote the following in longhand:

## Learning from a Hitchhiker

For years most of my travels had been business, driving to meetings or conventions, usually alone. It seemed odd to be going off to Detroit to spend a night with friends just for the fun of it. Without that destination in mind, I would simply have spent the weekend in my apartment, writing and grading papers.

Now I was speeding down Interstate 75 in the middle of a Saturday morning, talking to the red-headed hitchhiker I'd picked up just south of Flint. We both had Oakland University connections. I told her a college friend I hadn't seen for thirteen years was teaching there. She said I should drop down and just go sit in his class—it would freak him out. She laughed warmly imagining it. Then we talked about her travels.

She was on her way to Canada for the weekend, eager to get away although she had to be back on Monday. "Usually I'm living with some dude and can't really have a vacation," she said. "A friend of mine was going to go with me this weekend but his wife wouldn't let him. It's really a bummer." I nodded sympathetically and asked where she was going in Canada. She didn't know and somehow it came out that she was traveling on two dollars and thirty-five cents.

"Wait a minute, how can you afford to go to Canada on $2.35?"

"Maybe I'll get a gig in Windsor tonight playing piano." She shrugged. "Something will turn up. I just hope nobody hassles me. Usually nobody does."

A part of me inwardly dismissed her as a likable but flaky counter-culture type, but part of me who hadn't taken any vacation in at least four years was challenged. I wondered why I at age 36 had to wait and worry about finances and busywork and attention to unrewarding responsibilities while she at 22 or so could dare the world, unprepared, on $2.35. Perhaps she was foolhardy, but was I so afraid of life that I couldn't reach out for it without safety measures all around me?

When she saw the RenCen, she said it freaked her out. I dropped her near the tunnel to Canada, neither of us certain that she could cross there. I don't know if she made it back from Canada or not, but I know that two weeks later I was camping alone in the Leelanau Peninsula, all my obligations left behind for a weekend. I went to Sleeping Bear Dunes. It freaked me out.

When I read it through later I realized that some words and phrases in my journal entry had been used in the draft and that certain ideas—the sense of her personality, the idea of my not having vacationed and then going off on my own inspired by her example—and certain language had been important to get into the text. But I also realized that it was crammed with information and that it announced its theme rather than revealed it by the details of conversation and event. The draft might have been a rough draft or a first draft, but I decided to come at the telling a different way, by starting a whole new draft from scratch. This was a zero draft, a discovery draft, a writer-based draft that had revealed to me a number of things that were important to me about this experience but that no amount of revising would make into the text I hoped for. I had to start over, but I had a better sense of where to start from having done this preliminary work.

## The Importance of Preliminary Strategies for Drafting

Some preliminary strategies are chiefly ways to gather information; others are ways to focus on ideas. It helps to have a full repertoire of prewriting techniques to draw on as you need them and to use them to serve your own ends. Some strategies work better for material you are detached from, such as the research for a typical term paper, and other strategies work best for projects in which you need to get in touch with material you have already stored. In some cases you may even want to try two or three strategies on the same project—for example, clustering to give yourself ideas and then free writing to get into a more focused analysis. The point is to be able to get yourself started and to have some solid sense of what you are doing or what you can expect once you start drafting. Getting something on paper begins to clarify and define the work-in-progress and prepares the way for productive drafting sessions.

Depending on the writing occasion and project, the kinds of prewriting discussed here may be sufficient to produce a sense of where to start and where to go after you start. If the work is short enough, simple enough, or thoroughly rehearsed, and if the format and audience are familiar, it is possible to begin drafting and trust in the text you produce to generate the text you need to produce, more or less spontaneously. (We will say more about that in the next chapter.) However, it may be necessary to let these kinds of prewriting we have been discussing generate a preliminary plan of some kind. On a project using notes and research information, some sort of juggling of note cards into a specific (but tentative) order may be needed; the nice thing about note cards is that you can shuffle them around, lay them out on a table or floor, rearrange them, delete the ones that don't fit the emerging pattern of the piece, and organize the ones that do into an order you can follow like an outline. Another alternative is to create an outline, which can be either a sketchy general plan or a carefully crafted blueprint. These forms of prewriting not only prepare a writer to get started on the draft, but they can also guide the draft as it is being written. For that reason, we will look more carefully at these two forms of prewriting in the next chapter.

Holding off on the discussion of note card posting and outlining also gives me an occasion to iterate (or reiterate) that composing is not performed in simple self-contained steps. Just as string-saving and prewriting often occur simultaneously, so do prewriting and drafting. A simple sentence written down when a thought arises can survive from random string-saving through intensive revising, can even be the instigation of the entire work. For that reason, although engaging in prewriting of some sort is important, planning the draft in such detail that the drafting is essentially transcribing rather than composing usually isn't necessary—in fact, it may be impossible. Experienced wordsmiths try not to begin drafting before they are ready; prewriting, of whatever amount or scope, is chiefly a way of getting ready for drafting. Often a writer will discover at some point in the prewriting that she has been drafting as well, simultaneously. At that point she is ready to begin the drafting in earnest.

## The Wordsmith on the Word Processor:

### Starting

Starting a work-in-progress on the word processor isn't simply a matter of opening a new file, naming it, and beginning to type. Some hints about word-processing approaches to preliminary work have been given in the chapter, but this is a good place to review them and add some more.

**String-Saving Review.** Reviewing notes, journal entries, and other kinds of string-saving on the word processor gives you the opportunity to open a new file and copy and paste into it pertinent material from several sources. If the string-saving has been done in longhand or by highlighting photocopied material, this is a chance to record sources and copy material that might go into the paper. It is also a chance to organize or, as John Jerome refers to it, to catalog the material you have.

**Process Journal.** This is the time to talk to yourself in the journal about how you write what it is you know about the subject and the constraints under which the writing will be done, and predict where it might start and where it might go. This kind of talking to yourself often produces writing that you can copy and paste into a new file as a rough draft of a portion of the paper.

**Unsent Letters.** Like the process journal, unsent letters are a way of talking about what's happening in the work without getting in the way of doing the work by worry about composing a text. I like to start out projects in this way by pretending that I'm only explaining to someone else (who is always nameless in my letters) what I'm working on and what I might say about it. I fool myself almost every time. What I say in the letter, with some lines removed, usually becomes at least a small part and often a larger part of an early draft.

**Multiple Openings.** Some people suggest that writers should never write their introductions until after the rest of the paper is written, and I've recommended that earlier, but you have to start somewhere. The ease and speed of composing on the word processor makes it much more inviting to try starting out in several different ways. Spend ten or fifteen minutes trying to write as much as you can by introducing what you're going to talk about in the paper; then insert ten spaces and a page break or open a new file with a new title and try writing a completely different beginning, from a completely different perspective. If, for example, you're writing an essay about high school and your first opening begins with the first day you walked into the building, try writing another opening that starts when your name is called at graduation, or a third opening that begins right in the middle of the major event in the story ("I'd waited long enough and now I stopped the person

I had been longing to date just as she walked into the gym' or "How could Mr. Duffy say something so insulting to me in front of the whole class?"). In other words try out two or three different openings to the work-in-progress, print them out, and compare them with one another. Or open up different windows for each of them, make the windows small enough to place two or three on top of each other, and alternate reading them. Usually you find a beginning that you want to follow through on. If you have doubts, try sending the alternatives to other writers you are working with in a course chat group or by e-mail—or hand it to them—and ask which opening makes them most interested in what the paper might be about.

**Segment.** If you think you have a rough idea of the parts the work-in-progress is likely to have, make a rough outline. (For a paper on a water-skiing tournament, for example, segments of an outline might be "Beginning, Earlier Competitors, First Run, Second Run, Final Run, Later Competitors, Conclusion.") Use the return or enter button on the keyboard to give yourself some space in between the segments of your outline. Pick one segment to begin writing about, anywhere in the paper, knowing that you can change the outline, move back and forth among segments (paragraphs, parts, sections), and delete anything that does not need to be in the presentation text later in the process.

# 4

# *Drafting*

*You're learning about the thing you're writing about usually while you're writing about it. The writing of something will make you realize that there're pieces of it you don't get.*

—Connie Leas

A writer who has been regularly engaged in string-saving and who has recently engaged in prewriting the work she hopes to write is in a better position to begin drafting than the writer who suddenly realizes a deadline is nearly due and who begins examining the call for manuscripts or the class assignment in hopes of some clues about how to start a draft. The draft is something that comes out of the writer, not out of the assignment or the call for manuscripts, and the writer who has not been working on the project in some form before attempting a draft is either bluffing, trusting blindly in sudden inspiration, or simply confused about the process of writing. One of the chief causes of frustration in writing, including writing blocks, is premature drafting, which forces the writer to discover, plan, and compose simultaneously, a difficult enough task for an accomplished wordsmith, a discouraging and sometimes devastating one for an inexperienced writer. In writing, as in so many other things, readiness is all.

## The Advantages of Readiness

Readiness can help alleviate two common fears about drafting, the paltry draft fear, or fear of having nothing to say, and the dry well fear, or fear that "if we write what's in our heads, we will run out of words and ideas" (Warnock 309). To overcome the paltry draft fear we have to come to the drafting ready to lower standards and expectations, ready to accept the writing as incomplete, unpolished, uncertain; to overcome the dry well fear we have to believe that "writing can prime the pump instead of draining it" and that "the more the well is pumped, the greater the yield" (Warnock 309).

But readiness does not necessarily mean having a large block of time in which to complete the project in one sitting. Columnist Richard Reeves once went through a period in which he tried to complete long articles in a single composing session; he discovered that a reader could trace the flow of his energy in the articles, from his lively opening to his weary conclusions. An important part of drafting is recognizing that composing takes place over time—you can write separate portions on different occasions, allowing yourself to focus fully on one small task at a time, because you get a chance later on to revise the entire work. In the revising you can connect portions with logical transitions and arrange or rearrange sections to suit an overlying sense of structure. Depending on the project, such an approach uses the composing process to your advantage. If, on the other hand, you attempt single-sitting first-and-final drafts, you are imposing on yourself severe handicaps to successful completion of the project. Thus, a cardinal rule of drafting is: *allow yourself enough time, not only for initial drafting of portions, but also for the preliminary work and the revising;* a corollary to that rule is: *never expect to complete a writing project in a single sitting.*

## **D** *iscovery during Drafting*

Some of the reasoning behind these rules has to do with the nature of drafting itself. We have already discussed the element of discovery through writing, but in truth discovery is not something that happens only prior to drafting—it also happens during drafting. All the elaborate plot outline of a short story cannot keep characters from revealing unexpected facets of their personalities once the writer is trying to capture them on the page; all the careful listing of pros and cons for an argument you want to make cannot prevent you from stumbling on an unlooked-for weakness or serendipitous item of support in the course of explaining your position; all the clustering of reminiscences gathered as a preliminary to drafting a nostalgic essay cannot stop fresh memories from surfacing as you write about those you already recalled; all of the careful gathering of resources and assembling of quotes prior to writing a research paper cannot eliminate the recognition of the gaps in your information and understanding and the need for further research. The very act of drafting generates discovery; writing is never the mere recording of separately prepared thoughts. The experienced wordsmith knows and relies upon this aspect of drafting; the inexperienced wordsmith sometimes gets thrown by it.

Consider, for example, the nature of a zero draft, introduced in Chapter 3. A zero or discovery draft is a long way from the final draft, so much in need of revision that it barely counts as a rough draft. An experienced writer may launch into the writing of a zero draft without much concern for the direction it takes in order to use the draft as a means "to discover ideas that emerge at the ends of sentences, paragraphs, and papers" (Warnock 309). Perhaps the writing project is one where prewriting and planning of more structured kinds is less advantageous, such as writing a personal essay exploring feelings and memories. The zero draft is really a part of the prewriting rather than the drafting, because its function is chiefly to provide a text to work from in composing a rough draft. Even the much-admired essayist E. B. White claimed, "I always write a thing first and think about it afterward, which is not a bad procedure, because the easiest way to have consecutive thoughts is to start putting them down" (224–225).

The wordsmith writes a discovery draft willingly but tentatively, just to see what she has to work with; she knows she will better understand her point of view (or the nature of the story she has to tell or the argument that arises from the evidence she's gathered) once she has put something in writing. Annie Dillard, having written a discovery draft of an essay in her journal and having decided to work on developing it, took out some paragraphs immediately because they were

> the kind of absurdity you fall into when you write about anything, let alone yourself. You're so pleased and grateful to be writing at all, especially at the beginning, that you babble. Often you don't know where the work is going, so you can't tell what's irrelevant. It doesn't hurt to babble in a first draft, so long as you have the sense to cut out irrelevancies later. ("How" 17)

An inexperienced writer may produce a zero draft without recognizing it for what it is and attempt to treat it as if it were an advanced formal draft. Particularly when writers launch themselves out without much incubation and prewriting, the text itself determines its own development far more than it would if the writer had some sort of writing plan, no matter how sketchy. Often in such cases the constraints on the composing cancel one another out, so that uncertainty about the organization interferes with development of ideas and examples and expression of language. The discovery draft often produces a text that the writer can use to focus on structure later on or it can reveal problems of development that suggest ways of adding detail and illustration in a later draft. These are often the reasons an intended rough draft becomes a zero draft, because the issues of organization and development had not been resolved before the drafting began.

## The Shifting Concerns of Drafting Sessions

Organization and development are global concerns in a piece of writing; sentence structure and precise vocabulary are local concerns. The global concern with structure usually needs to be addressed before the local concern of style, not the other way around. In a draft it makes little sense to worry mightily over the exact wording of a section that structurally does not fit in the text. In the revision of an early draft (particularly a zero draft), many paragraphs get jettisoned to create a more appropriately balanced structure. It is easy to imagine the frustration of working on sentence level problems in those paragraphs only to have to throw them out because they really have nothing to do with the final topic of the paper. Sometimes, when a draft has been well prepared for and rehearsed, structure and style are created smoothly, simultaneously. More often, however, they have to be considered separately; when they are, structure usually takes precedence over style in the drafting and early revision stages.

Wordsmiths who understand the need for the writing to go through a process of discovery and change free themselves from the burden of inappropriate expectations. For example, David Denby, film critic for *New York Magazine,* doesn't worry about careful crafting or choosing exactly the right sentences in the first draft. Instead, he says,

> because I know I'm going to do another draft, I try to get it down on paper in the right order and get it to say more or less what I want it to say and not be too fussy about specific wording. (Root, *Working* 181)

When he comes to revise he does the work more willingly. He says,

> The second draft goes much more quickly and I find it very pleasurable. I find the first draft agony; the second draft I think is a lot of fun when you actually have something there to work with, to play with. It's at that point that your feelings of craftsmanship take over. (Root, *Working* 182)

Denby's experience is replicated by a host of other writers, all with their own variations of the process. The processes they evolve work specifically for them but may not work as well for—may even hamper— the composing of other writers. More important, they have developed strategies for dealing with the roadblocks that often emerge in writing. Revising is an important part of those strategies, because the reliance on revising for content, style, and expression frees up their concentration for the development and discovery of ideas earlier in the process.

Thus far I have insisted that the best approach to drafting is to come to it prepared to write and fully aware that it may take more than one session. By the same token, when you know you have to have another session, the best place to stop drafting is before you have run out of ideas. Try to stop when you still have something you want to add. Make a note of it or write a log entry about what you have to do next before you quit, but try to know what you will be doing at the next session. In other words, come to each drafting session prepared to write.

Experienced wordsmiths have noted that sitting in front of a word processor or typewriter or yellow legal pad, staring at the blankness and wondering for the first time what might fill it up, can lead to discouraging, unproductive sessions. You want to be able to get started as soon as possible at each session; coming prepared, even eager, to write is the best way to do it. Trust yourself that if you have something in mind, your subconscious will work on it for you in the interval between sessions and probably add to it, and when you do start drafting again, you will set the whole session in motion. Some wordsmiths have compared the process to pumping water from a well until it is low (never until it is dry) and then giving time for more water to seep in from the acquifer so that the well is full again the next time you need to use it. Several short composing sessions are often more productive than one long make-or-break session, because in the intervals between sessions, things happen to the ideas, to the language being rehearsed, almost despite the writer's intentions. By the same token, those composing sessions ought to be regular and frequent enough for you to maintain momentum on the project. Long layoffs between composing sessions on a single project interfere with the composing because you lose track of where you were and where you hoped to go, and searching for the lost thread of your earlier efforts wastes time and energy and encourages you to defer composing.

Just as short intervals in between sessions are valuable for the productivity of the sessions, so an interval between drafting and revising is valuable to get some distance, some perspective on what you have written. Never write and submit anything in white heat. Your closeness to the composing will encourage you to stay loyal to every word, every punctuation mark; ideas, because fresh, will seem exactly right. Giving yourself some time between drafting and revising helps you to be more objective about your writing; you forget what you had intended to say and have to deal with what you really said—not always the same thing. This is another reason for giving yourself enough time for a project— coming back to a draft after an interval of letting it lie, even if it is only a day or two, will give freshness to the reading and more effectiveness to the revision.

For the actual drafting itself, knowing the kinds of strategies that other writers use is helpful, but there are probably as many ways to draft texts as there are writers. Some writers need to curl up in a favorite chair with a favorite pen and legal pad for the rough draft; others use a typewriter and plenty of paper, X-ing out deletions and typing over changes; still others need the bouncing cursor of the word processor. Some insist on silence, some want specific kinds of "white noise" in the background, some can write no matter where or when. I use a variety of approaches, depending on what I'm writing, but often I like room to walk around in between bursts of drafting. Hemingway wrote standing up. Others can only write lying down. Whatever the place or the circumstances or the approach you take, it is a good idea to have a specific writing place and a block of writing time, even if it is only an hour or even a half hour. These help you stop yourself from doing other things that distract you from your writing. To help even further, these should be inviolable blocks of time, when the phone is unplugged or the door shut. Even small blocks of time, in a series, can produce good work over time.

# **W** *ays of Drafting*

So far as the actual drafting itself goes, that may vary with the project and the circumstances, but it probably ought to be consistent for the duration of the project and intended ahead of time. Following are some ways of drafting.

### **Free-Flow Drafting**

*Free-flow drafting* lets you start out from your string-saving and prewriting with at least a sense of where to begin and then lets your drafting follow the train of thought that the writing generates. This is an example of letting the text produced so far determine the text to be produced. In cases where the structure is fairly predictable (you have a thesis statement you will support with half a dozen arguments or you have a story to tell that is fairly simple) and where you've had plenty of time to incubate and rehearse, this can often produce a pretty usable draft. When I wrote short (three to four pages) essays for a local public radio station, I usually used this approach, because the length and the format were very familiar (I eventually wrote nearly 250 essays over eight years) and because I could use a casual style to talk about subjects on my mind. Most of them had been rehearsed in conversation or contemplation during walks to work or they grew out of things I had long mulled over in memory or recently reacted to strongly. My constant engagement with the essay series kept me continuously preparing to write, so the things I wrote about in a free-flow style were things ready to be written about. When I became too constantly engaged in experiences that didn't serve that form or allow that time for rehearsal and gestation, I had to give up writing for radio.

Free-flow drafting for a project based on research or critical analysis of other texts, as often is assigned in academic courses, ought to start after references have been collected, sources consulted, and notes reviewed. Considerable thought ought to go into the opening paragraph so that the text that emerges in the drafting starts in a place that promises connections to major ideas later on. Launching yourself into free-flow drafting for a project that depends on information outside yourself is obviously riskier than doing it on a project that depends on personal experience, knowledge, and memory.

The danger with free-flow drafting is that you might start the draft without sufficient string-saving and prewriting, in which case you'll produce a zero draft or you'll get launched on the draft and then flounder because you really had nowhere to go with it beyond the initial opening. Wordsmiths of long standing have file cabinets filled with false starts—that's no disgrace; but defeat can be discouraging, and unless you're willing to risk failure and willing to acknowledge and accept it (a good many failed student papers get submitted from a dogged unwillingness to throw out anything labored on), you would be better off trying one of the other approaches to drafting.

## Outlining

*Outlining* is a more traditional method and can be frustrating if you hope to follow it exactly and largely flesh it out with prose to make a paper. Tinkering with an outline can be part of the discovery process in prewriting, but often the drafting discovers new things that do not fit the outline. Instead, a rough outline can often be used as a general guide, a road map to where you are going and what you have to pass through to get there. For example, working on the armadillo assignment mentioned in Chapter 2, one student generated a loose outline that looked like this:

Name: "little armored thing" (Spanish)

Originated: South America. Now from Rio Grande to Oklahoma to Louisiana.

Food: Termites, scorpions, snakes

Armor: horny scales rather than hair. Fuse together to form shields over front & back. Midregion form jointed bands for flexibility. Protection from flesh-eaters.

Teeth: Order "Edentata," lack of enamel on teeth. Small, piglike, lacking roots.

Feet: Toes clawed for digging.

Breeding: Polyembryony. 4 identical quadruplets—division of single egg. 8–9 mo. gestation.

Species: 21–9-banded (Dasypus novemcinctus) only one in U.S. Smallest—fairy (Chlamyphorous) mole-like 5 in. (13 cm) Largest—giant (Priodontis) 5 ft. (150 cm)

Family: Dasypodiae 9 genera

Timid, nocturnal, bury themselves from pursuers

In drafting the piece, she would expand upon each of these items in order as she wrote, using the outline to determine sequence and following the hints accompanying the categories to assure her of covering what she felt were important points. The information in the last line was really separate from the outline, and she would attempt to use it wherever she could fit it in.

Another student working from the same sources gave herself a scantier road map:

Order—What it looks like/physical features/size—

What it eats

Where it lives

Mating habits

Its young

Ancestors

Kinds/best known

Folklore—literary connections

Life cycle

Because her outline is so sparse, she will essentially work on each section as a unit, referring back to the source articles and her notes, focusing only on the information needed for that section while she drafts. The outline is chiefly to remind her of the order of information; the drafting itself will arise out of the notes and sources.

One further road map: In this case the student has made an outline of the structure of the draft she intends to write, then left room to mention which subtopics within those headings she will need to address; to further organize them she put numbers in front of them to indicate the order she should follow and references to one of the three articles (A, B, or C) after them to remind her where to find the information when she needs it.

Armadillo

1. Where they are located

      Only 9-banded in U.S.

      So. America

2. Size/types

      p. C

      Species p. B

3. Body—

  "Make-up"[1.] p. A  [2.] underside, tail p. B

  as protection    [5.] tongue p. B

            [4.] snout p. C

            [3.] teeth p. C

  3A. What they eat Timid, nocturnal p. B

4. Breeding/Reproduction/Life Cycle

  p. B

  p. C unusual life cycle

5. Benefits

  p. C

  p. A eats termites & other insects

    incl. scorpions, also snakes

  p. B as food

6. Prehistory

  p. A

  p. B

7. Folklore p. A

8. Conclusion

To someone unfamiliar with the three articles, this outline only gives a rough order of general topics and provides no useful information about the subject, but it serves the writer herself very well because it categorizes and locates information and frees her up to deal with one element of this material at a time rather than making her hold it all in her head and juggle everything simultaneously.

An outline serves as an aid to drafting if you work on the outline before drafting and expect to change it as you write the draft. The outline needs to be flexible and fluid, changing and growing with your awareness of your text. It also helps you get some sense of proportion about the draft and alerts you when your train of thought has gotten derailed. When made after completing a draft, an outline is also a good way of finding out what you've said; numbering the paragraphs and listing their main contents in an outline can help you understand the flow of your ideas and the relative proportion of the elements. In any event, the outline has to be a flexible aid to drafting, not a rigid dictator of it.

## Note-Card Posting

*Note-card posting* is particularly useful for papers based on research, although it can also help any piece of writing in which there are pieces of prewriting that indicate sections of the proposed draft. John McPhee's method with notes is well known. According to William Howarth, McPhee takes a multitude of notes for whatever project he is working on and, when he feels he has enough, he "transcribes the notebooks, typing entries in order, occasionally adding other details or current thoughts as he goes" (McPhee xiv). He then photocopies that typescript and puts the original into a binder he can read through, at first perhaps making new notes and typing them up to add to the binder, then taking notes on patterns and possible structures. Once he has decided on the approach he will take to the subject, he codes the notes according to their topics and labels a series of index cards, which he sorts, arranges, and attaches to a bulletin board. In a sense he is making the outline of the article or book he intends to write; the index cards give him great flexibility in rearranging the structure.

McPhee then cuts up the photocopied set of notes and arranges the pieces by putting them in folders labeled in accordance with the index cards. He files the folders and then works on the writing by tackling the topic on each index card in order and consulting the corresponding file folder. "A large steel dart on the bulletin board marks his progress. He stabs the dart under an index card, opens a folder, further sorts scraps and ribbons until this segment also has a logical structure" (McPhee xv). It is an elaborate system for someone writing dense, complicated works, but it helps him break up the drafting into manageable sections and it helps him prepare for the drafting. As he has said, when the note cards are posted, "you're liberated now; there's nothing between you and the blank page" (Schuster). Working section by section he will produce multiple drafts to piece together as the work progresses. "You don't want something that's too finished or polished too early in the game," he says. "Learn to live with the rough drafts or else you'll produce no draft at all" (Schuster). People working on less ambitious projects can use the same system in a simpler way, by arranging note cards to produce a working outline—tacking them to a bulletin board, lining them up on a table, laying them out on the floor—and giving themselves a visual sense of the arrangement of the parts. At the same time it also almost automatically helps arrange the drafting into more manageable sections.

## Segmented Composing

*Segmented composing* is working on the project in sections, not necessarily in so systematic a way as McPhee's approach through note-card posting. As mentioned earlier, Richard Reeves's documentary film scripts are written a scene at a time, not necessarily in the order in which they appear in the final screenplay. Many writing projects can be broken into sections and the sections worked on out of sequence. In the social sciences, for example, reports on research often begin with a review of previous research followed by a section describing a specific research project, a section describing results of that research, and finally a section drawing conclusions or discussing implications of the results. Although there is a logical progression of the parts, the actual composition of each part need not follow the sequence of the final text.

John Jerome offers another example of segmented composing in his book *The Writing Trade,* where he describes how he established several computer files for a long magazine article on New Hampshire, typed his notes once on the word processor, and then moved or copied them into the appropriate files electronically. He explains:

> Those notes will be very rough; the job then will be to expand and develop the ideas in them, to put them into effective sentences, to try to make them fit the flow of the piece. When it comes time to write the text proper, I'll be pulling paragraphs out of the files and dropping them into place. If I get stuck—if I'm having trouble advancing the text or figuring out where to go with it next—I can always go to any of the five files and start sharpening the paragraphs there, before they're tossed into the text. That process usually generates enough new thoughts to get me going again on the piece itself.
>
> The power of this working method—for me—is that it lets me work as if the writing of the piece is just a case of cutting and pasting. It breaks into manageable pieces the otherwise daunting job of putting together a long, organized piece. When I lose headway in one place, I can always find someplace else to put my time until the next step makes itself clear. As a working method it is very self-protective, saving me from ever having to face a blank sheet of paper. (51–52)

In later stages of revision he can work on the connections between segments, the decisions about sequence, the elimination of repetition, the establishment of transitions, the introductory material for the piece he has actually written, and the concluding material appropriate for the segments that precede it.

## Incremental Composing

*Incremental composing* is more of a start-and-stop method of drafting that may begin from a point where the writer feels confident enough to start drafting but uncertain about direction and expecting the drafting itself to generate discoveries necessary for the composing to continue. One good example of incremental composing comes from Connie Leas, a technical writer who described her composing process for writing an instruction manual for a computer program: "My system would consist of: get an idea of the big picture, make an outline, then learn-write-revise-learn-write-revise until it's done" (Root, "Writing" 154). Having gathered a great deal of information and working from ever-changing outlines ("The more I'd learn about it the more I'd keep changing the outline"), she would work on sections of the program until she discovered information she did not understand, then either work through to an understanding or consult others who were more proficient with the program.

> You need to have an idea of the big picture but you can't begin to know all the details so what you do—what I do—is, just start. In the process I begin to learn. . . . You're learning about the thing you're writing about usually while you're writing about it. The writing of something will make you realize that there're pieces of it you don't get. (Root, "Writing" 154)

The work moves forward incrementally, growing with the writer's knowledge through the drafting itself.

## Page Guides

*Page guides* are used by some writers who have a sense of how long a piece will run to indicate what they ought to be writing about when they reach certain sections of the paper. *Detroit Free Press* columnist Jim Fitzgerald will write along the margin of a sheet of paper the relative positions of the topics he intends to address in his column-in-progress; he places the sheet on the desk beside his word processor and consults it as he types his first draft, adding or deleting items on the sheet as new or different ideas arise in the drafting. Richard Reeves has sometimes used the same approach on columns he has had to draft on legal pads, composing on a plane or in a hotel room. The notes in the margin remind him of the relative location of different items in the draft; because he knows from experience how the length of the longhand draft compares with a typed draft, he knows about where he needs to be making each of his points and starting to prepare for his conclusion. Like an outline or an arrangement of notes, the page guide is simply a way to keep yourself on track and prevent the text itself from taking over the composing process.

## Channeled Composing

*Channeled composing* is, in one sense, not unlike free-flow drafting, because both work their way through the text by letting the composing itself influence the direction of the text; but in another sense, it is the exact opposite, because it is carried out by careful, intense drafting that includes intensive revising. The drafting does not flow freely but rather is a constant endeavor to channel the flow of the text. Each sentence is worked on carefully before moving to the next, and then when the next is completed, the two together have to be examined before moving on to a third. Particularly when the ideas in a text have been thoroughly rehearsed (in thought or in prewriting activities) this approach to drafting can be effective in carefully constructing the text. Annie Dillard writes,

> The reason to perfect a piece of prose as it progresses—to secure each sentence before building on it—is that original writing fashions a form. It grows cell to cell, bole to bough to twig to leaf; any careful word may suggest a route, may begin a strand of metaphor or event out of which much, or all, will develop. Perfecting the work inch by inch, writing from the first word toward the last, displays the courage and fear this method induces. (*Writing* 15)

The free-flow approach assumes you can always go back to it and revise; the investment is not so great that you feel you have to protect it at any cost. The channeled approach gambles that you can get through this in one controlled draft, and sometimes the gamble pays off. Often, however, especially for inexperienced writers, it doesn't. As Annie Dillard *also* observes,

> The reason not to perfect a work as it progresses is that, concomitantly, original work fashions a form the true shape of which it discovers only as it proceeds, so the early strokes are useless, however fine their sheen. Only when a paragraph's role in the context of the whole work is clear can the envisioning writer direct its complexity of detail to strengthen the work's ends. (*Writing* 16)

In practice, then, the first six approaches are safer strategies.

# C hoosing among Drafting Strategies

These drafting strategies are not mutually exclusive; all can be used in combination with one another. The strategy you use may be the one that seems to work the best for you or, more likely, the one that seems to work the best for the writing you have to do. Personal narratives, for example, are often easier to draft in a free-flowing style than a library research project or a formal report, because they are essentially stories about what happened, and the major focus of the draft is chiefly getting the details in the proper order with the appropriate balance between them; the other two types of projects involve collecting data from other sources, analyzing and rearranging it, and figuring out a way of presenting it to a reader that clarifies the relationships among the bits of information. Such a project may call for more structured approaches to drafting. Experienced wordsmiths know that they can draw upon a range of writing strategies as the need arises and circumstances invite. Elaine Maimon, an academic writer, says,

> I find that my writing practices vary within a single project and, more particularly, from project to project. Sometimes I start writing a draft without a specific plan in mind. More often, I have a shopping list of points I wish to cover or images I want to invoke. Once in a while, I make an outline from rough notes. I deem myself to be an experienced writer because I have learned flexibility and the capacity for systematic variability. (142–143)

The number of sessions that a writing project demands also depends on the nature of the writing project. Obviously it is better to plan for more sessions rather than for less, particularly if you are working toward a deadline. Discovering that you don't need all the sessions you had scheduled yourself—because the work is going better than you anticipated—is preferable to discovering that you will need many more sessions than you predicted—because the work is not going well. In addition, the number of sessions may depend on how much string-saving and preliminary work has already been done, how familiar you are with the material you're writing about, how accustomed you are to the format you intend to be writing in—it may depend, that is, on how ready you are to start drafting.

# E *xamples of Drafting*

### The Hitchhiker Essay

The piece that I had begun to work on about the hitchhiker, introduced earlier, proved to be a challenging little essay, in part because of the limits imposed on it by the place I hoped to submit it. I needed to tell the story, create her character and my conflict, give a sense of place, and keep it all within 450 words. The journal had recorded my initial meeting with her and my strong reaction; the discovery draft had revealed to me certain things I wanted to get across—her personality, my timidity as opposed to her adventurousness, the likelihood that this encounter prompted me to do my first solo camping trip. But the discovery draft was not acceptable as a rough draft of the essay—it didn't create character as much as I wanted, it explained too much and showed too little, it didn't get across the contrast between us and my eventually adapting her attitude the way I now knew I wanted. So I started over from scratch with a new draft, which ended up being the draft I would revise through to publication (see Figure 4.1). In this draft I tried to show everything through the conversation and then toward the end get around to the idea of my initial reaction to her and my eventual venturing out on my own. Because this piece is so short it was easy to work through a draft in a single sitting. The discovery draft was pretty much free-flow composing; this draft is more controlled, sort of semichanneled composing—a general sense of structure was mapped in my head, and I took some pains to direct the drafting to cover the ground I now realized I wanted to cover.

### Research on Book Reviews

In the chapter on string-saving we looked at a grid that a writer researching critical reviews of a biography of C. S. Lewis might have made to organize the material. While that grid was constructed specially for this book, we can examine drafts of a paper actually written from those resources.

Melody, the author, had collected several reviews of *C. S. Lewis: A Biography* by A. N. Wilson; she had been motivated to report on reviews of this book by the nature of the assignment and also by having read and enjoyed books by Lewis. Although the instigation for the research and the resulting paper came from her professor, the actual subject of the paper came out of her own interests and

~~There was something anachronistic about the red headed young hitchhiker, something hippylike and out of the Sixties.~~ The red-headed

young hitchhiker, ~~casually wearing a~~ *dressed in* tee-shirt and jeans, *a duffle bag at her feet,* had the flaky

serenity of a flower child. She was cheerful and chatty from the moment

I picked her up *on I-75* South of Flint. When we passed the exit ~~on I-75~~ for

Oakland University, I told her a friend of mine from college, whom I

hadn't seen for thirteen years, was teaching there. She said I ought to

find out when his classes met and just go sit in one . "It would really

freak him out," she laughed.

I laughed with her, as much at her pleasure at imagining Football's

response as at the thought of surprising him. She was an interesting,

open person, a pleasant surprise for someone who had expected to be

traveling alone. ~~I had been bound for Grosse Pointe, feeling odd about~~ *I was on my way to Grosse Pointe to stay overnight with friends*

~~staying overnight with friends and leaving my schoolwork behind;~~ *but I felt guilty about the stack of ungraded papers*

~~much as I~~ I'd left behind in my apartment, ~~driving like someone late for~~

~~an appointment, when~~ and I continually caught myself driving with the

grim determination of someone late for a business meeting. It was

dawning on me that I seldom left home for any reason that wasn't

~~motivated~~ *somehow connected* with my teaching.

My hitchhiker had had different reasons for not traveling as much as

she'd like. "Usually I'm living with some dude and can't really have a

vacation." The irony ~~of that~~ was that one of them now was wandering

around all over the Western United States while she was still in

Michigan, working part-time as a musician. But she took disappointment

lightly, accepted it with only a few words of regret. "A friend was going

to travel with me this weekend but his wife wouldn't let him. ~~What a~~

~~bummer.~~ *It's really a* bummer." I nodded sympathetically.

**FIGURE 4.1** *Rough Draft*

She was on her way to Canada for the weekend. ~~I asked~~ but when I asked her ~~where~~ what city, she didn't have a destination in mind. I said I'd let her off near the tunnel where she could catch a ride or maybe walk across.

"Is there a toll? Do you think it's more than $2.35?"

"I don't even know if you can walk across. Why did you say '$2.35'?"

"Because that's all I have with me."

"How can you afford to go to Canada for a weekend on $2.35?"

~~"You're going to Canada for the weekend on $2.35?" The Dutch uncle in me was struggling to reach the surface. I restrained him and~~

"Oh, I'll probably get a gig in Windsor tonight playing piano." She shrugged. "Something will turn up."

We were pretty near the Ren Cen. She said that it freaked her out. I dropped her near the tunnel to Canada, neither of us certain that she could cross. ~~She slung~~ Her duffle bag over her shoulder, her thongs slapping on the pavement, she strode off one way to unplanned adventure and I drove off the other ~~way.~~ to my safe haven in Grosse Pointe.

I wanted to shake my head and write her off as ~~a~~ either pleasantly dizzy ~~flower child and~~ or unbelievably ingenuous. But something in me was challenged. I wondered why I at age 36 had to wait and worry about finances and attention to unrewarding responsibilities while she at 22 or so could brave the world unprepared on $2.35. Perhaps she was foolhardy but was I so afraid of life that I couldn't reach out for it without safety measures all around me?

Two weeks later I ~~was~~ camp·ed alone on the Leelanau Peninsula, all my obligations left behind me for a weekend. I fell asleep to the sound of Lake Michigan and strolled beaches and woods like a vagabond. I even climbed Sleeping Bear Dunes. They really freaked me out.

**FIGURE 4.1**   *(continued)*

background. Having read Lewis (but not Wilson's biography) she was in a position to be more knowledgeable about what she read; she was interested in comparing the reviews as a way to decide whether to read the biography (a common motive for reading reviews in the first place). On the photocopied reviews she underlined key sentences or put a brace (}) in the margin identifying material she might use in the paper. Later she went back through the reviews and identified sections she intended to use by writing "quote" next to the brace. With the reviews spread out before her to consult, she wrote what she identified as the zero draft of the paper, the draft in which she would discover what she had to work with.

The reviews of the book "C. S. Lewis: A Biography" by A. N. Wilson held mixed reactions. The book gives people a look inside the life of the English writer who wrote such things as "The Chronicles of Narnia," "The Great Divorce," "Surprised by Joy," and many other works.

One important comparison in the reviews of this book was that between Wilson and other authors who have written biographies of C. S. Lewis. One critic claims that Wilson's biography is "clearly the best" but is "not without its difficulties" (Riga 116). Riga states that the biography by R. L. Green and Walter Hooper tended to make some of the more important aspects of Lewis's life seem less important and that of William Griffin failed to write about new material that he had discovered (116). Another critic explains that even though Wilson had not had the personal acquaintance with Lewis that previous biographers (such as Sayer, R. L. Green, and Hooper) had, he does a good job regardless of this with his "detailed, intimate knowledge of two major factors in Lewis's life—Oxford University and English literature" (Aeschliman 54). Yet another critic of Wilson's book is not so generous with praise. Gilbert Meilaender believes that the best biography of Lewis is the one by George Sayer and that Wilson's is "heavy on information, but with almost no interpretative schema" (525).

One agreement among the critics is that the book lacks logic and believability. One says that the biography "shows certain signs of haste" and that parts of the book that Wilson thought to be most important are hard to understand (Brookhiser 62). Another critic made it seem like Wilson was in a hurry to finish, causing serious oversights (Meilaender 525). Meilaender also says that "The longer one ponders Wilson's narrative the more difficult it becomes to grasp its logic" (528). Riga explains that Wilson's ideas are highly speculative and that he has taken many risks in these speculations that "seem ill-advised or just plain wrong" (116). John Elson also briefly mentions speculations that Wilson has made (A3).

Many of the critics mention several faults in the biography that cause them to question its validity. Meilaender explains that what is unique about Wilson's book is that he attempts to analyze the psyche of Lewis, but that Wilson also fails to support his ideas with sufficient factual evidence. When talking about the way that Wilson analyzes Lewis in search for an understanding of him and his relationships with women, the critic says that his evidence used to support his ideas "can't carry the interpretive load Wilson places upon it. The threads form an informative and witty narrative, but the facts do not fully persuade" (Meilaender 528). Riga maintains that the arguable judgements made about Lewis in Wilson's biography were highly speculative and that the risks he took will lead readers to question the validity of the book (116).

The more convincing critics are the ones who do not care for Wilson's biography of Lewis, such as Meilaender. They seem to be more educated with the life of Lewis and offer more information to support their claims. Many of these critics do not agree with Wilson and the way that he attached so much significance to events in Lewis's life that seemed illogical. They also agree that he is guilty of overinterpretation of what made Lewis act in the manner in which he did and write what he did.

The fact that Melody labels this draft a zero draft tells us she knows she is on a voyage of discovery here, trying to put into her own words the ideas she has found on the pages of the reviews and trying to quote the reviewers directly when it seems important to let them speak for themselves. Some of the language is awkward and some of the ideas vague, but in a zero draft she does not worry about that—those things can be addressed and resolved during revisions to follow. For the present she needs to assess what she has and make some decisions about how to work with it. In the next chapter we will see some of the ways Melody revised this draft.

# D *rafting and Other Elements of Composing*

At least one more thing needs to be said about drafting, and it relates back to the constant subtext of this book—that we are not talking about discrete, distinct stages of writing in each chapter but rather about certain moments of concentration on various strategies for composing. Throughout the drafting you may find yourself planning and preparing, on the one hand, and revising, on the other. After all, your plans are not set in concrete and your revisions don't have to—can't—wait until the drafting is done. That being the case, you may consider a draft completed when you feel you have to focus on it in a different way than you have been so far, when you feel instead that you ought to go back over the whole of it and make it come together better (revising), or when you feel you ought to work on its appearance and eliminate stumbling blocks to comfortable reading of it (editing or proofreading).

This may not require a complete draft, however. In many academic papers, for example, the ideas you need to present in the final section of the paper or the conclusion depend so much on the clarity and logic of the evidence you have presented that you simply *cannot* write the conclusion until you have revised the central section. By the same token, it is often difficult to write the beginning of the paper until the rest of the paper is substantially finished, because the beginning section of a paper introduces the reader to the ideas that make up the rest of the paper. Laboring on the introduction can be frustrating because you may not know enough about the content you're trying to introduce and won't until you've discovered or learned more by trying to write about it. Conclusions are easier to write—they conclude the paper you've already written. Introductions are harder—if written first, they introduce the paper you hope to write, the one that may have to change the most as drafting opens new doors. (Once, clearing out my filing cabinet of fifteen years worth of old drafts, I discovered that most of my energy in revising went into the first half of my papers.) Sometimes it is better to launch yourself into the center of your paper first, work it through, then write your conclusion, and finally write your introduction. When that is the case, clearly a draft can be considered only a substantial section of the paper, not a complete version of the entire work.

Thoreau once observed in his journal that, in a writer's first attempt to write on a subject, "he produces scarcely more than a frame and groundwork" because "each clear thought that he attains to draws in its train many divided thoughts or perceptions." For this reason,

> the writer has much to do even to create a theme for himself. Most that is first written on any subject is a mere groping after it, mere rubble-stone and foundation. It is only when many observations of different periods have been brought together that he begins to grasp his subject and can make one pertinent and just observation. (11: 438–39)

The prudent wordsmith, then, approaches drafting as an opportunity to discover the foundation she will build on, takes a flexible position concerning the progress of the work at hand, and does not expect to work on the finishing touches of the edifice until she is certain that what she is building is solid enough outside to support the interior walls that demand more painstaking work.

## The Wordsmith on the Word Processor:

### Drafting

Drafting on the word processor is like drafting anywhere else, especially if you start at the beginning, go to the end, and make revisions later on. The ability of the word processor to effortlessly delete, insert, replace, and move text gives it an edge over other ways of composing that require more clerical labor. A few ideas to try include:

**Outlining.** The word processor, like a pad and pen or a typewriter, lets you create an outline as a road map or guide. The handy thing about the computer, however, is the way it lets you fill in the outline. Because you can move the cursor to any place in the outline and create space to write in, you can work on various parts of the whole as you get ideas. If you create the outline and save it as "Outline," then duplicate that file as "Paper" and begin filling in the outline, you have the markers for the way in which you expect that paper to go together. If the text you compose makes you see better ways of structuring the paper, you can change the outline by replacing, adding, deleting, or moving sections. When you fill in the outline to your satisfaction you can delete the outline itself, and you have your paper ready to revise, tighten, or connect through revision. (This is essentially how I've been composing these word-processing pages.)

**Segmenting.** John Jerome's idea of creating several files among which to shift your attention is particularly good for works-in-progress that are composed partly from other sources or have distinct sections. Sometimes the progress on a work grinds to a halt because the writer doesn't know where to go with the section being worked on; this approach lets the writer skip to another section, saving the transition or connection or further development to work on later. Then cut and paste commands can put the segments together as a whole.

**Copying.** When I am working on a project that uses research, I now try to carefully copy quotations and information accurately in one or more research files. I attach to my information an accurate reference to the source, but I also copy that reference and paste it in a separate file for works cited or works consulted. This is an act of string-saving, but when the drafting starts I can go to those files and copy material easily to transfer to my draft. At the end of the draft I can also go through the list of references and simply delete the ones that didn't get used in the paper, then copy those works cited to the last page of my draft. I'm shuffling fewer papers this way, keeping an accurate record of my sources, and saving time on my copying. Since most professionals who write tend to go back to the same sources, I have an ever-growing list of resources already prepared to select from in future work as well—I will not have to type this information again and again, each time risking mistakes. And if I have to delete quotations or references in later drafts, I have not lost them forever—they are still available in another file.

# 5

# *Revising*

*I find that I can criticize my composition best when I stand at
a little distance from it—when I do not see it, for instance.*
—Henry D. Thoreau

*Revising,* like composing itself, is most successful when the writer
has a clear, practical model of it to direct him. When the model is
inaccurate or irrelevant, successful revising is impossible. Often,
particularly among novice writers, revising is confused with transcribing, editing, or proofreading, and subsequently such writers
tend to do those tasks instead of actually revising. By *transcribing* I
simply mean copying the text over neatly; *editing* means going
through a text carefully, line by line, to examine the sentence structure, the grammar and usage, the clarity and accuracy—the last
time the writer wrestles chiefly with expression of ideas; *proofreading* is the review of the final copy to make certain that it contains no
errors in text preparation, such as misspellings, typos, misnum-
berings, inconsistent documentation, and the like. All three of these
tasks are usually necessary to complete a writing project by preparing a *presentation text* of the work (something we will consider in
the next chapter), but they are also all tasks that, by and large, can
be performed by someone other than the writer. Magazine and
book publishers routinely employ typists and typesetters, editors,
and proofreaders expressly for these purposes, although writers
themselves should make their best efforts at these tasks before submitting final copy. However, transcription, editing, and proofreading are almost wholly about correction; revising is about rethinking
and potentially making substantial changes in structure or sense. It
is about looking at the text you have composed, whether an initial
draft of the whole work or a significant section of it, in search of
ways to review, reconsider, or perhaps replace and reformulate it.

# The Differences between Drafting and Revising

Revising does not mean starting from scratch all over again. Throwing out everything you have done and beginning anew produces a first (or rough or zero) draft, not a revision. The revision retains what is working in the earlier draft and eliminates and replaces what isn't. The ability to revise—and the willingness as well—is central to becoming an accomplished wordsmith. Annie Dillard in *The Writing Life* compares a writer facing a draft that isn't working with a builder examining a house that isn't being constructed the way it should (4). The builder hopes that, if anything has to be removed, it will be a decorative wall, not a bearing wall holding up the whole structure; but even if it is a bearing wall that has to go and the whole edifice has to be torn down to the foundation, the builder has to be willing to do it. So too must the wordsmith treat none of the writing as indispensable, preservable at any cost; in the end it is the soundness of the edifice that matters, not the ease or speed of its construction. Much that is weak in the final draft of a piece of writing comes from either the writer's reluctance to remove it or her inability to recognize that it needs removing.

For that reason the advice in the Chapter 4 about letting the text sit for a while before attempting revision is an important one. (Try reading a paper you wrote a year or two ago and you'll see what I mean.) Time off gives you the distance you need to see your work from the perspective of someone else; some of the prose will surprise you because you won't recall having written it. That gives you the chance to be objective about it, less committed to every aspect of the work you have completed. You will more easily see the need for revision if you yourself have difficulty following your argument or understanding an example or untangling the syntax of a sentence. The time away from your writing does not allow your mind to cover for your confusion the way it does when the reading immediately follows the writing. Equally important, even as the time off helps you identify weaknesses, it also makes it possible for you to identify strengths you might otherwise overlook or discard inadvertently. You have a better sense of what is working and what is not. Depending on the complexity of the project, in most early drafts not everything is working equally well.

Patricia Hampl, an essayist and memoirist, has observed about revising, "It still comes as a shock to realize that I don't write about what I know: I write in order to find out what I know." She notes that readers often do not realize "the enormous degree of blankness, confusion, hunch and uncertainty lurking in the act of writing." In well-written prose, we readers have "the lovely illusion that the words ... must also have been written exactly as they appear, rhythm and cadence, language and syntax, the powerful waves of the sentences laying themselves on the smooth beach of the page one after another faultlessly." But that is not how the words get to the page for any writer. The reality is closer to Hampl's own experience composing.

> But here I sit before a yellow legal pad, and the long page of the preceding two paragraphs is a jumble of crossed-out lines, false starts, confused order. A mess. The mess of my mind trying to find out what it wants to say. This is a writer's frantic, grabby mind. (97–98)

Even experienced wordsmiths can be frustrated by the hope that one day the words will come out without needing to be revised, but they simply have to recognize that they won't.

Some writers have years to work on projects and some of them never actually get around to completing them—there is no pressure to do so. Student writers, by contrast, have lots of pressure on them to finish their writing tasks hurriedly. Consequently, they tend to opt for first-and-final drafts, revising while drafting rather than stepping back from the draft. The result often is work that simply isn't as good as it could be (which actually can be more disappointing than work that isn't as good as the teacher wanted it to be). But even in the rushed climate of college, a little planning can give the writer a little time off to get away from the draft, if only overnight or for a few hours. You can complete the paper before you go to bed, then sleep on it and revise it in the morning. Often your subconscious continues working on the paper and the revision comes more easily. Or you can complete the paper in the morning and give yourself until evening before you revise it. Any gap between drafting and revising works to your advantage. Ideally, you ought to shoot for an interval of a few days or a week, and even confer with the teacher or other students about a particularly difficult work in progress; but if the reality of the school environment prevents this, even a little time off can help.

I do not mean to suggest that drafting and revising are totally separate tasks—drafting involves constant revision, revision often demands extensive new drafting—but I would encourage most writers to plan specifically for revision in the time they allot to their writing. When revision is performed as a new action after you have more or less completed a draft, instead of as a subprocess of drafting itself, the revising task changes. You finally get a chance to work on the piece as a whole rather than as an emerging portion.

## A *pproaches to Revision*

To begin with, give yourself some time in between drafting and revising, as little as a couple of hours, as much as several days—whatever it takes to get some distance from it and let the heat of creating cool. If you can work from clean copy, so much the better. It may vary for the individual writer, but generally an early draft with all its changes, strikeovers, crossouts, and inserts can be difficult to envision as a total work; the labor of following its circuitous trail without getting sidetracked by dead ends can be an act of labyrinthine concentration that diverts attention from the entire design. The reason so many wordsmiths have converted to word processing, either entirely or in concert with manuscript or typescript, is simply that it makes the scribal portion of composing less laborious and painful and produces clean, readable copy so easily. The advantage of having a printed text to work on lies in the opportunity to see it fresh, as another writer might encounter it. Some writers revise directly on the video display terminal, some only by hand on hard copy, some both ways; I recommend working on hard copy at least once during revising—the contrast with the way the text looks on the screen is often revealing—and always before the final printing of presentation text.

One common way to revise is simply to begin at the first sentence of the draft or of the section that would come earliest and to read it carefully with a colored pen in hand (so that changes stand out against the black typeface of the hard copy), making changes as you go along. Particularly with a late or reasonably advanced draft, this method is likely to work well; it is especially useful as a strategy to edit rather than revise. But it is a problematical approach with an earlier draft, because it focuses attention on the text only at the sentence or paragraph level rather than on the whole work. Certainly at some point a writer has to attend to the ways the sentences go together, one after another, but there are more systematic strategies to choose from that engage the writer with the subject, format, and occasion for writing.

## Assess What You Have Accomplished So Far

To begin with, you need some way of assessing how well your current draft achieves what you hoped it would. Rather than turn to the draft itself, it is often useful to step back from the draft and do some prewriting about the revision. Thoreau suggests such an approach when he writes in his journal:

> I find that I can criticize my composition best when I stand at a little distance from it,—when I do not see it, for instance. I make a little chapter of contents which enables me to recall it page by page to my mind, and judge it more impartially when my manuscript is out of the way. (Stapleton 115)

Without looking at the text itself, he attempts to think it through again, and the mental manipulation of the contents makes him think about structure and content without being inhibited by the actual draft.

## Outline the Draft

One variation of this might be to actually make up a rough outline of the contents by going systematically through the text, forcing yourself to struggle with the ways the parts relate to one another. Annie Dillard writes, "If you are used to analyzing texts, you will be able to formulate a clear statement of what your draft turned out to be about. Then you make a list of what you've already written, paragraph by paragraph, and see what doesn't fit and cut it out. . . ." ("How" 17). As an example of how this might work in practice, consider the following drafts of a student paper.

FIRST DRAFT

### How I Gained Self-Confidence through Water-skiing

1    When I was about twelve years old I began to get this complex that I was no good at anything. I had absolutely no self-confidence. My little brother is one of those people that is good at almost anything that he does. He is especially good in sports, which is where my complex came from. Ever since he was about ten, he has been able to beat me in almost anything. If he would play any sport—tennis, racquetball, ping-pong, badminton, or

any other sport—he would beat me. I was always trying to find things that I was better in than he was. I never could find anything until I found that I had a real talent in waterskiing. It was from my first waterskiing tournament that I lost that lack of self-confidence.

2      It was the summer of 1979. My family and I were spending the summer up north at our cabin. I had wanted to enter a water-ski tournament for quite a while, but it wasn't until the summer of '79 that I seriously started to think about it. A friend of mine told me about the tournament about three weeks before it was to take place. So, now I had no excuse not to go, except for three obstacles I would have to overcome. They were first, I had to overcome my nervousness and trying to talk myself out of going. Second, I had to get the O.K. from my parents. And third, I had to get the day off. Now that wasn't going to be an easy task, since the place I was working was a canoe livery and our heaviest business was on the weekends, and the tournament was on a Sunday.

3      The first problem of trying to talk myself out of going wasn't too hard to overcome, because I really wanted to go ski in the tournament. I did, however, try to talk myself out of going a few times. But they were all unsuccessful because of my desire to go.

4      The second barrier wasn't so easy. Since I only had my license for a couple months my parents weren't very confident in my driving. They didn't want me to make a three hour drive to Grand Rapids by myself. After that I thought all had failed. Then, later that night a friend from home called to see if he could come up and visit some time, and by coincidence he was free the weekend of the tournament. So that was great, I had someone to ride with me. My parents didn't think it was so great though, but after some persuasion they said that I could go.

5      Then came the worst problem of the three. It was the one that I feared the most. In fact, I almost talked myself out of going because I was so scared to ask my boss for a Sunday off. I thought it would be no for sure, and it wouldn't be worth wasting my time or his. I went and asked him two weeks in advance. Although he wasn't happy, when he found out why I wanted the day off he said go right ahead. I just about fainted when I heard him

say yes, because it was such a surprise. I hit cloud nine when he answered me.

6      When I went home my parents were as shocked as I was and started to reconsider, but I told them that they were backing out of their end of the deal. So they said I could go.

7      I began to practice every day before I would go to work. And if it was still light out when I came from work, we would go out for a few runs. When I had bad runs I would get discouraged, and try to talk myself out of going because I just knew that I would get beat.

8      As the tournament got closer I got more nervous. I started to try to talk myself out of it more and more. I began to make up excuses for not going. Excuses like, it's a long way to drive just to go skiing. I'll have to get up really early, I would save everyone at work a lot of problems if I didn't go, and so on. I told myself that I've come this far I'm not going to turn back now. That was the only thing that kept me from not going.

9      The day before the tournament finally came. I came home from work just dead on my feet. I had planned on going to bed early, considering that I had to get up at five o'clock in the morning to leave for the tournament. To my misfortune some other friends of mine from home decided to come up and surprise me. Not knowing what I was doing the next day, they asked me to go see a movie with them. I got home at about eleven thirty and again I started to talk myself into not going because I would be so tired that I wouldn't be able to ski well at all. Again I overcame my anxiety.

10     We got up at five o'clock and took off. When we were about five miles away from home I remembered that I didn't fill the car up with gas. When I looked at the gauge I only had a quarter of a tank. We went back and siphoned gas out of my friend's car. It gave us half a tank, and we left in hopes of finding an open gas station. Luckily as we were passing through a small town at six o'clock, a gas station was just opening. So my worries were all over.

11     We got to the tournament site without any further problems. Except, I was so nervous I could hardly talk. I kept picturing myself falling just as I was getting up. This was typical of how I thought then. I always pictured myself doing the worst possible thing.

12    I got positioned about tenth out of thirty. As I watched the other skiers go out and make mistakes I became a little more calm. When my turn came I was so nervous I wasn't able to speak. My concentration was at a peak. When I got done I was in first place. I couldn't hardly believe it. I watched the others as they came closer and closer to my score. Nobody reached it though. I had won my first tournament.

13    I was finally really good at something. Better than everyone else. Although I didn't go down to the tournament to prove myself, I had. I came home with the first place trophy to the surprise of many.

14    This incident was one of the most important parts of developing my self-confidence. This one in particular because it was the first, but two other tournaments that summer and a couple last summer have helped me gain amounts of confidence in myself. I found that with this boost of confidence I'm doing better in everything that I do. I'm doing better in school. I even give my little brother a hard time in the games that we play. It was because of this first ski tournament that I've gained confidence in myself.

By numbering the paragraphs and listing their contents in order the writer sees a pattern in the paper:

1. General introduction of problem: Competition with brother, self-doubt; specific introduction to tournament
2. Introduction to tournament decision; introduction to three obstacles
3. Obstacle 1: Nervousness and self-doubt
4. Obstacle 2: Parents
5. Obstacle 3: Day off from work
6. Obstacle 2 again: Parents
7. Practice; Obstacle 1 again: Nervousness
8. Obstacle 1 again: Nervousness
9. Obstacle 4: Late night with friends
10. Travel to tournament; Obstacle 5: Gasoline
11. Arrival at tournament; Obstacle 1: Nervousness
12. Competition in tournament: Early skiers, my runs, later skiers, victory
13. Victory and what it meant to me
14. Conclusion: Victory and what it meant to me; competition with brother, self-confidence

The first draft essentially runs from stream-of-consciousness, a form of free-flow composing. The author is following the chronology of events, from the earlier lack of self-confidence and the initial decision to enter a waterskiing tournament through competition and victory in the tournament and the subsequent gaining of self-confidence. Because he starts the paper so far back in time, he finds himself considering the minor problems of preparing to attend the tournament rather than the actual competition. The sentences come out as they occur to him, and he repeats words, phrases, and ideas a great deal because he has not discovered the best way to express his ideas. The first and last paragraphs are connected by the references to competition with the brother and the change from self-doubt to self-confidence, but the twelve paragraphs in between do not really focus on the achieving of self-confidence. In fourteen paragraphs only one, the twelfth, is really about the tournament.

Looked at in this way the author can recognize the balance between the parts in the structure he has produced and discover that while his intention might have been to write a paper recounting how he gained self-confidence, his actual accomplishment has been a draft recounting how he overcame obstacles to get to his first waterskiing tournament. Before he does anything much with individual sentences, he has to decide what the structure of the paper is to be: does he want to change this to a paper on how he got to the tournament? does he want to keep the problems of getting there and expand the tournament section to be most important, doubling or tripling the length of the paper? does he want to focus on the tournament and jettison the obstacles to getting there?

Compare the first draft with the second. Here the student writer condenses seven paragraphs into one, abbreviates one paragraph of irrelevant travel details into a single sentence, and expands that single paragraph on the tournament into six paragraphs of description of the competition. It is now a paper about how he gained self-confidence through waterskiing.

SECOND DRAFT

## How I Gained Self-Confidence through Water Skiing

1       When I was about twelve years old I began to get this complex that I was no good at anything. I had absolutely no self-con-

fidence. My little brother is one of those people that is good at almost anything that he does. He is especially good in sports, which is where my complex came from. Ever since he was about ten, he has been able to beat me in almost anything. If we would play any sport—tennis, racquetball, ping-pong, badminton, or any other sport—he would beat me. I was always trying to find things that I was better in than he was. I never could find anything until I found that I had a real talent in waterskiing. It was from my first waterskiing tournament that I lost that lack of self-confidence.

2    I had always wanted to enter a waterski tournament, but had never seriously considered it until the summer of 1979. A friend told me of a waterski tournament, and said that I should enter it. The tournament was about three weeks away, so I had no reason for not going. Except in the past I had had this problem of talking myself out of things like this. This time I wasn't going to let that happen, although I came close a couple of times. Also, my parents weren't going to be too keen on the idea of me driving three hours to Grand Rapids by myself, since I only had my license for a couple of months. Luckily a friend decided to go with me. So after a little persuasion, my parents decided to let me go. One last problem I was going to have to face was, I was going to have to get the day off. I thought for sure that I wouldn't be able to, but much to my surprise, when my boss heard what I wanted the day off for he said it would be no problem. I began to practice as hard as I could. Many times I became discouraged, and would start cutting myself down, saying I would get beat, and it was stupid of me to even go. This was typical of the way I thought back then. Because of the way I was thinking I started to make excuses for not going. Excuses like, I'll have to get up really early, it is a long way to drive just to go skiing, and things like that. When I would catch myself thinking like this I would try to stop, and start thinking positive. It must have worked because I never successfully talked myself out of going.

3    Tournament day finally came and with great amounts of difficulty and anxiety, we made it down to the tournament on time to get registered.

4    I was picked to be tenth out of about thirty skiers. As I watched the first nine skiers go out and make mistakes I began to calm down a bit. As the first person went I thought that

he must be one of the worst, and everyone was going to beat him. As the other skiers went I saw that it wasn't that the first skier was all that bad, because all the skiers were like that, it was just I had higher standards. I began to believe that I could do good in this tournament if I didn't make any serious mistakes. It was that thought of making a mistake that was making me nervous now.

5      As the boat pulled me out of the water I had a feeling of confidence like I had never had before. My concentration was higher than it ever was before. As I pulled across the wake and through the entrance gates, I knew it was going to be a good run. I can usually bet that if I don't get through the gates good then it will be a bad run, and if I get through them good then it will be a good run. Compared to my practice runs, I made it through the entrance gate perfectly. At this point I knew that if I could just make it around the first buoy I would be alright. I always seemed to have problems on the first buoy in practice. Once around the first buoy, the others came with great ease. I was relaxed as I went through the course. I had never been so relaxed before. Once I was through all six buoys I was shocked. It had never been so easy. It was almost too easy.

6      As the boat turned around to come back through, I was thinking that the speed the boat would be speeding up to was a speed that I never had made it through at before.

7      As I pulled through the entrance gates I almost fell. I began thinking, oh no it's going to be a bad run. Once around the first buoy everything was under control. Now I had five more to go. I began to ask myself if I could do it and set a personal record. As I rounded each buoy I was amazed at how easy they came compared to practice. It wasn't easy, but I was smooth and under control. I finally made it around the sixth buoy. I was in shock. I had set a personal record, if nothing else.

8      As the boat was turning around to pull me through again I began to see what a little confidence could do. As I came toward the course I decided to go for it and try to shatter my old record. It turned out that I fell going around the first buoy. It didn't really matter though. I had done better than I thought I would ever do. Also I was eleven buoys ahead of the second place person. I did realize, however, that twenty people still had to make runs. I still had confidence that my score would hold up.

9    As I watched the other skiers go, I realized they weren't any different than the first bunch of skiers. Although a couple skiers came close to my score, none of them beat it. I had done better than I ever expected to do both in the score that I received and in my placing. I had outscored the closest person by four full buoys, and that is quite a bit.

10    I was finally really good at something. Better than everyone else. Although I didn't go down to the tournament to prove myself, I had. I came home with the first place trophy to the surprise of many.

11    This incident was one of the most important parts of developing my self-confidence. This one in particular because it was the first, but two other tournaments that summer and a couple last summer have helped me gain amounts of confidence in myself. I found that with this boost of confidence I'm doing better in everything that I do. I'm doing better in school. I even give my little brother a hard time in the games that we play. It was because of this first ski tournament that I've gained confidence in myself.

A number of points need to be made about this revision. First, we need to notice the structure that emerges in the second draft.

1.  General introduction of problem: Competition with brother, self-doubt; specific introduction to tournament
2.  Introduction to tournament decision; introduction to three obstacles: Nervousness and self-doubt, parents, day off; practice and nervousness
3.  Travel to and arrival at tournament
4.  Early competitors
5.  My first run: Part 1
6.  Turning around for the 2nd part of my first run
7.  My first run: Part 2
8.  My second run and final score
9.  Later competitors; victory
10. Victory and what it meant to me
11. Conclusion: Victory and what it meant to me; competition with brother, self-confidence

Clearly this is now a paper focused on the waterskiing tournament. The first draft turned out to be essentially a zero draft; the second is a rough draft of the paper that will eventually emerge from the assignment. Although he might have written the rough draft without having done the zero draft if he had done a sufficient amount of prewriting and planning, all the evidence of the zero draft suggests that the paper was done without planning and entirely in a single sitting. (That's why the tournament itself is described so quickly—the writer has spent two pages getting to the tournament and proportionately should spend about five more describing the competition; instead he hopes to end on the third page and cuts the story short to do it.) But the zero draft may have been necessary just to give the writer something to work from, some general mass of material to reshape—a discovery draft can help you discover what you don't want in the paper as much as what you do want.

Another point to be made is that this outlining reveals problems of structure and suggests ways of reorganizing the paper. Because he ends up condensing paragraphs 2 through 7 into one new paragraph 2, throwing out paragraphs 8 and 9, reducing paragraph 10 as paragraph 3, and expanding paragraph 12 into paragraphs 4 through 9, it has been unnecessary for him to worry very much about the sentence-level revisions the original draft might have needed. Now that he has settled on a structure in the second draft, he can begin to focus on sentence-level revisions: eliminating repetition, adding details of description and narration, smoothing unwieldy phrases, clarifying transitions—all the work that makes revision so rewarding and that in the zero draft would not have solved the problems of structure. It is still a very rough draft, but he has given himself a good base to work from.

## Write a Journal Entry

Another strategy to assess what you have accomplished so far might be to react to the draft by writing a log entry or a journal entry, talking to yourself about what you hope to accomplish and what you think you have accomplished so far. Often these kinds of dialogues with yourself can lead you to work through problems of structure, arrangement, logic, or emphasis. When you do go back to the actual draft, you may have a clearer sense of how to revise it. As an example, note this journal entry written after an early draft of a paper recalling a student's performance on stage in high school and what it meant to her to be able to perform in front of hundreds of people.

## JOURNAL ENTRY

As I read my paper, I see that I could add better transitions between paragraphs. I could do this by telling what else is going on besides what I am doing. I could tell about the other acts and how I felt watching them.

I could also add more detail about how I felt during the song and the other reactions I had to the audience.

I could tell how I had to get a certain mental state to do this—and to keep from laughing.

Overall, a little more detail about my performance on stage and a little more explanation of how I felt would be beneficial to this paper. I am happy with how it has come along so far but I would like to be able to show the reader exactly how I felt so that they could be more involved.

Writing the journal entry gives her some specific tasks to attend to in the revising. In addition to logs and journal entries, unsent letters can also be helpful because attempting to explain to someone else what you're up to forces you to find other ways of expressing your ideas, which in turn helps you get a handle on them.

### Talk about It

Conversation can help with revising whether or not the other person gives any advice or even reacts at all. Sometimes all we need is a sounding board, a sympathetic ear toward which we can direct spontaneous, extemporaneous reflection. Explain to someone else what you've done in the paper, what you hoped to do, what you might do to revise it. You can also talk to yourself, as Nancy Sommers says she does:

> Between drafts, I take lots of showers, hot showers, talking to myself as I watch the water play against the gestures of my hands. In the shower, I get lost in the steam. There I stand without my badges of authority. I begin an imagined conversation with my colleague, the one whom I told in the parking lot of the grocery store, "Oh, but you must read Foucault." I revise our conversation. This time I listen . . . (28)

The talking will generate realizations about ideas, language, perspective, structure, organization, and content of the draft that mere solitary, unspoken, or unwritten reflection will never do.

## Engage the Work as a Whole

Once you have assessed what you have accomplished in some way and return to the draft itself, try to engage it as a whole work (even if it is only a loose assemblage of parts at the moment). There are a number of ways to do this:

- Read the draft aloud all the way through, from start to finish, stopping only to make check marks where something sounds wrong or seems unclear or does not work. In both "global" structural matters and "local" stylistic matters, oral reading often exposes difficulties that silent reading overlooks, particularly in regard to the sequencing of ideas and the clarity of sentences. If you have difficulty following the train of thought or the syntax in certain places, obviously you will need to attend to them in revision.

- Have another person read the draft aloud to you while you jot down your reactions to what you hear. Afterward, read your list of the things you noticed to your reader and see if that person has anything else to add that he noticed trying to read it orally. This strategy obviously would work well with a fellow writer or a classmate with whom you could reciprocate by reading his writing aloud.

- Read the draft through silently, making notes in the margins where you feel particular attention will need to be given later on and identifying the kind of attention you think it will need. Bracket or cross out sections you think might be dropped altogether.

- Read the draft through silently, numbering the paragraphs in order and jotting down a phrase or sentence that summarizes what each paragraph is about (as we did with the water-skiing drafts). If you can quote a sentence or a portion of a sentence from each paragraph, so much the better. Afterward, use the numbered list of jottings to draw up an outline of the draft you have actually written. Ask yourself if the pattern that emerges makes sense to you, if the balance between paragraphs is appropriate and desirable given the subject you are working on and the point you want to make, and if the weight of individual sections is proportionate to the overall structure.

All these strategies review the text as a whole and prepare you for revising. You can use more than one of them on a draft and also react to these preliminaries in logs or journals before beginning to revise. By reviewing the draft before revising you discern areas that need attention and are able to break down the task of revision into specific, local subtasks. Of equal importance, you get a sense of what *doesn't* need to be accomplished, either because it's fine as it stands or because it should be discarded rather than revised.

The question of overall structure is important. It makes sense to work on larger issues before working on smaller ones; close and painstaking revision of individual sentences is a waste of time if eventually you have to throw out the entire page. Realistically, of course, one has to expect that sometimes the pages you work hardest at simply have to be discarded in the end, and at those times often it is the hard work itself that makes you realize that. Still, if you can concern yourself with organization and development at the beginning, you can often reduce unnecessary revision of individual sentences.

# **W** *hat to Attend to in Revision*

However you approach your initial review of the draft's structure, there are virtually universal elements to attend to.

- Make certain you understand the organizing principle of the draft, the reasons behind the decisions you have made about what material has been included and the order in which it has been presented. Writers tend to include elements for a host of reasons that do not always serve the overall structure or the general point of the draft. Essayist Noel Perrin once pointed out an item in an essay of his that was not important information for the general reader or a vital contribution to its theme but had been included in hopes that one potential reader might react to it; it was worth it to him at that point to insert something unrelated to his organizing principle. The point is to know why certain elements have been added and whether they support or conflict with the central principle. When you know that, you can decide what to keep and what to discard or replace. One way to confront the organization is to reorganize: describing the need to overcome the "hypnosis" of his own voice, John Jerome says, "I sometimes read the pages out of order, even read the sentences in reverse order—from the bottom of the page up—just to jar myself out of this overfamiliarity" (111). On the computer he will sometimes move sentences around, seeing if they will go better elsewhere (38); other writers cut up sections of a typed or longhand draft and shuffle their reading sequence in order to discover what differences different structures make, which is preferable, and which parts seem superfluous or irrelevant.

- Make certain that the beginning and the ending of a piece are both related to the material in the center. One way to do that is to read the piece through, then reread the beginning immediately. Usually the beginning and the ending ought to be connected in some discernible way, whether tightly or loosely. Often it is clearer how the beginning or the ending is related to the center because the center leads *from* the beginning and leads *into* the ending, but it may be less clear how the beginning and the ending are related to one another because the nature of the center has changed in the drafting. More often than not, the beginning needs to be revised to make it better prepare the reader for the center and the ending; as Annie Dillard says, "Usually I end up throwing away the beginning: the first part of a poem, the first few pages of an essay. It's not holy writ" ("How" 17). But it can also happen that the draft has gotten away from the writer and diverged from a beginning that was preferable to the piece as written; in that case the center and ending will need the major work. In essence there are three questions to be answered here: Does the beginning really begin the draft you actually wrote? Does the ending really end the draft you actually wrote? Are the beginning, the center, and the ending all vitally linked parts of a focused whole?

- Make certain that the center of the piece is sufficiently developed. Clearly I am speaking in the most general terms here, but development is a relative matter. Compositions can be overdeveloped, underdeveloped, or balanced, and the question of appropriate development depends on the topic, the constraints on text form and length imposed by submission guidelines or assignment requirements, and the audience you hope to reach. In the waterskiing drafts, the description of the tournament in the first draft is undeveloped, and the description in the second draft is more thoroughly developed. Generally the questions to ask yourself are, first, whether the information provided is appropriately detailed and concrete for the depth in which you intend to treat the subject and to which the reader needs to be taken and, second, whether the development is sufficient to support the assertions you make, ideas you propose, or conclusions you reach. As before, you need to look at the center for its relationship to the beginning and the ending.

- Make certain you understand the sequence of the development and the ways ideas, paragraphs, and sentences are related to one another. In the main this is the task of examining transitions and connections, the phrases and sentences that link ideas or lead from one paragraph to the next. Ask yourself whether the reader can see why this particular paragraph follows the preceding one or why this particular sentence is succeeded by the one following it. It may mean looking at individual paragraphs and determining their structure, shifting some around to make the development of ideas clearer or smoother or more logical, and eliminating, adding, or replacing some paragraphs. (For an example of shifting the position of paragraphs, see Figure 5.1, later in this chapter.)

- Make certain you are satisfied with the way each sentence sounds. To get the sound of the sentence you may have to read it aloud to a real or imaginary listener. If you have any doubts about whether that listener can follow the sense and the syntax (structure) of the sentence, work on the sentence to make it clearer. Most wordsmiths argue that changes in style are usually changes in content for them and generally that's true. The more you work on making certain your sentences make sense, the more likely it is that they will be clear and correct syntactically. Much murkiness and error on the sentence level is the result of murkiness on the conceptual level. One way of getting at the conceptual level is to consult other readers; technical writer Connie Leas, as she worked on a computer-program instruction manual, often went to experienced users of the program to check with them about whether her descriptions and instructions made sense or were easy to follow, then used their reactions to guide much of her revising. Other writers simply have to write down various versions of a sentence in order to see how it looks on the page and then pick the version that best does the job.

■ Make certain that you keep coming back to the entire composition. All the components of the draft should serve the composition in its entirety. The more often you keep yourself in touch with the whole piece, the more the work on its parts will connect with the whole.

■ If you make extensive revisions to a draft, prepare a new, clean copy and read it through carefully to make certain you understand the revisions and have actually deleted and added the portions of the text you meant to change. Revisions can become confusing and lead to strange text. A concluding sentence of my book on Thomas Southerne reads: "No *really complete* understanding of Restoration drama, particularly in the 1690s, can be *complete* without reading his work . . . " (italics added); I had intended to change "can be had" in the original to "can be complete" and "no really complete" to "no real" ("No really complete understanding . . . can be had" to "No real understanding . . . can be complete"), but fumbled the alteration in execution and am permanently stuck with a mutant version in print (128). A careful final reading of clean copy uncovers many such errors in transcription.

To follow through on some of this general advice, you might look back at the two drafts of the waterskiing paper in this chapter or ahead to Chapter 7, where we will follow a couple of wordsmiths through work on a single project. For the present we can also consider two other samples, one a revision of a research paper carried through several drafts, the other a revision of an essay we have followed through several chapters.

## T he Growth of a Research Paper

We can see something about the nature of progressive revision in the following series of excerpts from the paper describing critical reviews of *C. S. Lewis: A Biography* by A. N. Wilson. A portion of the research information on the subject appears in Figure 3.4 in Chapter 3; an early draft of the paper appears in Chapter 4. To gain some understanding of how a writer discovers ideas and grows in confidence and ability in the process of revising a paper, we can follow a key section of Melody's paper through multiple drafts.

## Examining Revisions in a Key Section

In the middle of her earliest draft (she calls it her zero draft) she included the following paragraph:

> One agreement among the critics is that the book lacks logic and believability. One says that the biography "shows certain signs of haste" and that parts of the book that Wilson thought to be most important are hard to understand" (Brookhiser 62). Another critic also noticed signs of haste when it became apparent that Wilson had only mentioned Lewis's most powerful book twice, which made it seem like Wilson was in a hurry to finish, causing serious oversights (Meilaender 525). Meilaender also says that "the longer one ponders Wilson's narrative the more difficult it becomes to grasp its logic" (528). Riga explains that Wilson's ideas are highly speculative and that he has taken many risks in these speculations that "seem ill-advised or just plain wrong" (116). John Elson also briefly mentions speculations that Wilson has made (A3).

The paragraph was a place to bring together references to the believability and logic of Wilson's book, and in her second draft, she left the paragraph exactly the way she had written it while she concentrated on other aspects of the paper. But when she began to revise the second draft, she realized that not everything in the paragraph dealt with believability and logic and that she needed to separate her ideas a little more. In the third draft she wrote:

> One agreement among some of the critics is that the book seemed to be written in haste. Brookhiser noted that some parts of the book that Wilson thought to be most important were not explained well, and therefore hard to understand (62). Another critic also noticed signs of haste when it became apparent that Wilson had only mentioned Lewis's most powerful book twice, which made it seem like Wilson was in a hurry to finish, causing serious oversights (Meilaender 525).
>
> Another problem often mentioned by critics is that of believability and logic. Riga explains that Wilson's ideas are highly speculative and that he has taken many risks in these speculations that "seem ill-advised or just plain wrong" (116). John Elson also briefly mentions speculations that Wilson has made (A3). One critic says that "the longer one ponders Wilson's

narrative, the more difficult it becomes to grasp its logic" (Meilaender 528).

She had realized that some of the comments were really about the perceived hastiness of the book rather than believability and logic and therefore created two paragraphs where she had had one.

Throughout the revision process she kept talking to other group members in the class about her paper and kept going back to the original collection of reviews to keep checking how she was using quotes and paraphrases with her own original sentences. This led her to see that the question of tone had come up in the reviews and that she had ignored it so far, so in her fourth draft she pieced in a paragraph on tone after the one on haste, the best place for it to go in her view. She also decided that believability and logic as she was using the terms really referred to the same thing and made the last paragraph in this sequence only about believability. In the fifth and final draft she changed two sentences a little and prepared a presentation text that read:

One agreement among some of the critics is that the book seemed to have been written in haste. Brookhiser notes that some parts of the book that Wilson thought to be most important are not explained well, and therefore hard to understand (62). Another critic also noticed signs of haste when it became apparent that Wilson had only mentioned Lewis's most powerful book twice, which made it seem like Wilson was in a hurry to finish, causing serious oversights (Meilaender 525).

Two critics state a specific problem with the tone. Brookhiser says that "too often his tone, which is meant to be conversational, slides into chattiness" (62). Another critic says that Wilson's book is enjoyable to read, but his tone often becomes "snide and condescending" and that "very few people are mentioned without that tone of voice creeping through" (Meilaender 528).

Believability is the major area of concern that troubles the critics. Riga explains that Wilson's ideas are highly speculative and that he takes many risks in these speculations that "seem ill-advised or just plain wrong" (116). Another critic also mentions Wilson's theories about Lewis's personal life (Elson A3). Riga states that these arguable judgments made about Lewis in Wilson's biography will lead readers to question the validity of the book (116).

Her progress through this section of her paper illustrates her progress through the entire paper and through other papers in the course, the slow build-up of detail through reinterpretation and shuffling of the parts to get a better sequence of details and a more thorough and accurate reading of her source materials. Without the continual rereading and revising, her paper would have been shallower and the information she gives about critical reaction to the biography less comprehensive. Her work on revision helps her understand what she's writing about as well as make it clearer and more detailed for a reader.

## Examining Revisions in the Opening

We can also see the changes wrought in the way Melody begins the paper. The opening paragraph is always tricky in a piece of writing. The writer learns so much about the topic through drafting and revising, but the opening paragraph is usually written before discovery through writing begins. By the time the key sections of a paper have gone through several drafts, the introduction often no longer "introduces" the ideas in the paper. Melody keeps revising the the opening paragraph to keep it current with the revisions in the rest of the paper. As a different way of examining this part of her work-in-progress, look at the parallel texts in Figure 5.1, where four different drafts are laid out in pairs. (I've included the first sentence of the second paragraph of each draft as well.)

In the first two drafts the changes Melody makes to the first sentence are both stylistic and concerned with focus. She inserts a new second sentence in the second draft that makes the opening paragraph more about the critical reaction to the book and shifts the major emphasis of her report from the subject of the book to reviews of it. In both drafts the first sentence in the second paragraph remains the same—she has yet to work on the connections here.

In her third draft she makes the opening sentence much more direct about what her findings will be. She switches around the second and third sentences of the second draft and rewrites them to make the second sentence connect to the subject of the book before the third sentence directs the reader toward the focus of the reviews. She also changes the opening sentence of the second paragraph, making it flow more smoothly.

By the fourth draft Melody has established the first two sentences of the opening paragraph, but writes a new third sentence

| First Draft | Second Draft |
|---|---|
| The reviews of the book "C. S. Lewis: A Biography" by A. N. Wilson held mixed reactions. The book gives people a look inside the life of the English writer who wrote such things as "The Chronicles of Narnia," "The Great Divorce," "Surprised by Joy," and many other works.<br><br>One important comparison in the reviews of this book was that between Wilson and other authors who have written biographies of C. S. Lewis. | The critical reaction to the book <u>C. S. Lewis: A Biography</u> by A. N. Wilson was mixed. The critics who reviewed the book were most interested in the believability of it and how it compared to earlier biographies of Lewis. The book gives people a look inside the life of the English writer who wrote such things as "The Chronicles of Narnia," "The Great Divorce," "Surprised by Joy," and many other works.<br><br>One important comparison in the reviews of this book was that between Wilson and other authors who have written biographies of C. S. Lewis. |
| **Third Draft** | **Fourth Draft** |
| The critical reviews of the book <u>C. S. Lewis: A Biography</u> by A. N. Wilson were both positive and negative, although the more convincing critics were those with unfavorable reviews. The book attempted to probe into the private life of C. S. Lewis in order to analyze the events that shaped his life. The critics were primarily concerned with the believability of the book and whether or not Wilson gave sufficient evidence to support his views.<br><br>One common topic in the reviews of the book is the comparison between Wilson's biography and other authors who have written about C. S. Lewis. | The critical reviews of the book <u>C. S. Lewis: A Biography</u> by A. N. Wilson were both positive and negative, although the more convincing critics were those with unfavorable reviews. The book attempted to probe into the private life of C. S. Lewis in order to analyze the events that shaped his life. It also works to persuade the intellectuals who have put Lewis aside to re-examine him ("Beer and Beatitudes" 81).<br><br>One common topic in the reviews of the book is the comparison between Wilson's biography and those of other authors who have written about C. S. Lewis. |

**FIGURE 5.1** *Revisions of Opening Paragraph*

that substitutes a reference to the critics' reaction for one about the critics' concerns. This allows the opening sentence of the second paragraph to introduce the issue of comparison with other biographies. The issue of believability, which had been the topic of the third sentence in the third draft, is one we have already seen developed further in the middle of the paper.

Changes have been occurring throughout Melody's paper over the course of several drafts. In the fourth draft Melody works on making transitions tighter and sentences clearer and more direct. She only tinkers with the beginnings of a few paragraphs to make the transitions clearer before running off this draft as her fifth and final draft. It reads:

## A Report on the Reviews of "C. S. Lewis: A Biography"

The critical reviews of the book <u>C. S. Lewis: A Biography</u> by A. N. Wilson were both positive and negative, although the more convincing critics are those with unfavorable reviews. The book attempts to probe into the private life of C. S. Lewis in order to analyze the events that shaped his life. It also works to persuade the intellectuals who have put Lewis aside to re-examine him ("Beer and Beatitudes" 81).

One common topic in the reviews of the book is the comparison between Wilson's biography and those of other authors who have written about C. S. Lewis. F. P. Riga claims that Wilson's biography is "clearly the best" but is "not without its difficulties" (116). He also states that it avoids the faults of other biographies, such as that of R. L. Green and Walter Hooper, which tended to make some of the more important aspects of Lewis's life seem less important, and that of William Griffin, who failed to write about new material that he had discovered (116). Another critic explains that even though Wilson had not had the personal acquaintance with Lewis that previous biographers had, he does a good job with his "detailed, intimate knowledge of two major factors in Lewis's life—Oxford University and English literature" (Aeschliman 54). Yet another critic of Wilson's book is not so generous with praise. Gilbert Meilaender believes that the best biography of Lewis is the one by George Sayer and that Wilson's book is full of puzzling judgments that he has "pondered several times but remain[s] unable to fathom" (525).

One agreement among the critics is that the book seems to have been written in haste. Brookhiser notes that some parts of the book that Wilson thought to be most important are not explained well and are therefore hard to understand (62). Another critic also noticed signs of haste when it became apparent that Wilson only mentions Lewis's most powerful book twice, which made it seem like Wilson was in a hurry to finish, causing serious oversights (Meilaender 525).

Two critics state a specific problem with the tone. Brookhiser says that "too often his tone, which is meant to be conversational, slides into chattiness" (62). Another critic found Wilson's book enjoyable to read, but felt that his tone often becomes "snide and condescending" and that "very few people are mentioned without that tone of voice creeping through" (Meilander 528).

Believability is the major area of concern that troubles the critics. Riga explains that Wilson's ideas are highly speculative and that he takes many risks in these speculations that "seem ill-advised or just plain wrong." Another critic also mentions Wilson's theories about Lewis's personal life (Elson A3). Riga states that these arguable judgments made about Lewis in Wilson's biography will lead readers to question the validity of the book (116).

There are also other faults in the biography that cause them to question its validity. Meilaender explains that what is unique about Wilson's book is that he attempts to analyze the psyche of Lewis, but that Wilson also fails to support his ideas with sufficient factual evidence. When talking about the way that Wilson analyzes Lewis in search for an understanding of him and his relationships with women, the critic explains that the evidence used to support his ideas "can't carry the interpretive load Wilson places upon it. The threads form an informative and witty narrative, but the facts do not fully persuade" (528).

Brookhiser says that there is a problem with Wilson's point of view. Wilson writes that the most attractive Lewis is the author of <u>English Literature in the Sixteenth Century</u>. Brookhiser disagrees sharply with him and says that "that book, like all of Lewis's criticism, is as fresh and sharp as Wilson says it is; but to be attracted to it primarily is like focusing on Mozart as a Mason, or Sir Arthur Conan Doyle as a table-rapper" (62).

Overall, the critics agree that the book is lively, readable, witty, and pleasurable to read. However, the more convincing critics are the ones who see past this and realize that there are many faults in Wilson's book that cannot be overlooked. These critics seem to be more educated in the life of Lewis and offer more information to support their claims. They do not agree with the illogical way that Wilson attaches so much significance to events in Lewis's life in order to demystify his personal life and beliefs. "The longer one ponders Wilson's narrative, the more difficult it becomes to grasp its logic" (Meilaender 528).

Works Cited

Aeschliman, M. D. "Getting the Core." Rev. of C. S. Lewis: A Biography, by A. N. Wilson. National Review 30 April 1990: 52–57.

"Beer and Beatitudes." Rev. of C. S. Lewis: A Biography, by A. N. Wilson. The Economist 3 March 1990: 81.

Brookhiser, Richard. "Seeking Faith." Rev. of C. S. Lewis: A Biography, by A. N. Wilson. Commentary May 1990: 61–62.

Elson, John. "Love's Labor." Rev. of C. S. Lewis: A Biography, by A. N. Wilson. Time 5 March 1990: A3.

Meilaender, Gilbert. "Psychoanalyzing C. S. Lewis." Rev. of C. S. Lewis: A Biography, by A. N. Wilson. Christian Century 16 May 1990: 525–529.

Riga, F. P. Rev. of C. S. Lewis: A Biography, by A. N. Wilson. Choice September 1990: 116.

Throughout her revision process, Melody kept returning to her original sources, selecting new quotes to replace some she had already used and using what she had written as a way of checking on what she had read. At the same time, the revisions kept refining what she was saying, helping her to discover new associations of ideas and to sort through the material she had already assembled in order to present it more logically and more clearly. At that point she also went back to the photocopied reviews and the information she assembled about them to generate her "Works Cited" list in conjunction with the handbook assigned to the course. This is the presentation text she turned in.

# R *evising the Hitchhiker Essay*

The hitchhiker essay began as a journal entry and progressed through several drafts. The final draft emerged from an important round of revision (see Figure 5.2).

This draft has undergone one further set of revisions by hand from the draft in Chapter 4; this example is the typed version of that third draft with a fourth set of revisions in longhand. I had dropped the first title, "Learning from a Hitchhiker," as too dull, adopted "The Hitchhiker's Travel Guide" as a kind of catchy play on *The Hitchhiker's Guide to the Galaxy,* then playing on local radio, and then settled on "Traveling Without Baggage," because it was richer and more ironic—the hitchhiker was physically traveling light (without luggage) and metaphorically traveling light (with-

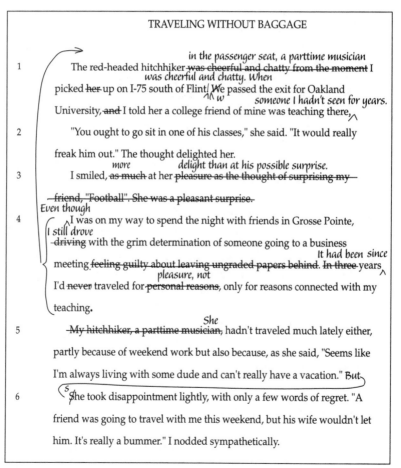

TRAVELING WITHOUT BAGGAGE

1 The red-headed hitchhiker ~~was cheerful and chatty from the moment~~ I *in the passenger seat, a parttime musician* *was cheerful and chatty. When* picked ~~her~~ up on I-75 south of Flint. We passed the exit for Oakland *someone I hadn't seen for years.* University, ~~and~~ I told her a college friend of mine was teaching there,

2 "You ought to go sit in one of his classes," she said. "It would really freak him out." The thought delighted her.

3 I smiled, ~~as much~~ at her *more* ~~pleasure as the thought of surprising my~~ *delight than at his possible surprise.* ~~friend, "Football". She was a pleasant surprise.~~

4 *Even though* ∧I was on my way to spend the night with friends in Grosse Pointe, *I still drove* ~~driving~~ with the grim determination of someone going to a business *It had been since* meeting. ~~feeling guilty about leaving ungraded papers behind. In three~~ years *pleasure, not* I'd ~~never~~ traveled for ~~personal reasons~~, only for reasons connected with my teaching.

5 ~~My hitchhiker, a parttime musician,~~ *She* hadn't traveled much lately either, partly because of weekend work but also because, as she said, "Seems like I'm always living with some dude and can't really have a vacation." But

6 She took disappointment lightly, with only a few words of regret. "A friend was going to travel with me this weekend, but his wife wouldn't let him. It's really a bummer." I nodded sympathetically.

**FIGURE 5.2** *Revised Draft*

out baggage), and by the end of the piece I too was traveling without cares and responsibilities. Moreover, I had realized that this was the theme of the piece, the organizing principle: I wanted to show how this hitchhiker made me realize that I could be more free, less controlled, about enjoying experience. To do that I wanted to give readers a sense of her personality in contrast to mine and a sense of the change in my outlook to be more like hers—that's why I adopted her phrase ("They really freaked me out") at the end of the piece.

In this typed draft I have an introductory section that gets the reader immediately in the car meeting the hitchhiker and seeing my reaction to her (paragraphs 1, 2, 3), a section about my attitude toward travel (paragraph 4), a section about her attitude toward travel and vacations (paragraphs 5 and 6), a section about her current trip (paragraphs 7 and 8), a section in which we go our separate ways and a comparison is made between us (paragraphs 9 and 10), and a conclusion in which I reveal a change in my attitude and

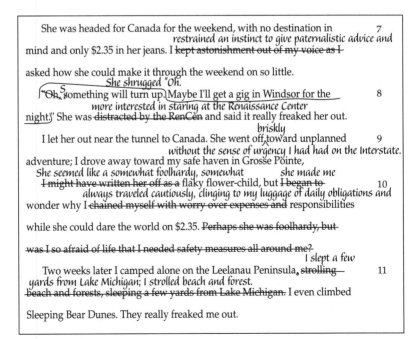

**FIGURE 5.2**  *(Continued)*

outlook (paragraph 11). In longhand I marked a shift that moved paragraph 4 ahead of the first three paragraphs, because I wanted to present the hitchhiker without that interruption and make the opening paragraph more of a contrast both with the paragraph that closes the part where she travels with me and also with the concluding paragraph. It also occurred to me that paragraphs 5 and 6 went together as one paragraph because of their unity of focus. Some of the sentence changes are additions of detail in order to be more specific (paragraph 4: "and I felt guilty about leaving ungraded papers behind") or clearer about what was happening (paragraph 9: "without the sense of urgency I had had on the Interstate"). Some changes were to alter the response the reader might have; saying in paragraph 8 that "She was distracted by the RenCen" seemed more negative an image of her than "She was more interested in the Renaissance Center"; saying in paragraph 7 "I kept astonishment out of my voice" didn't explain what I was feeling or make enough contrast between us, so I changed it to "I restrained an instinct to give paternalistic advice," which also made me seem a stuffier, more mature person than she was, an image I wanted to convey. Paragraph 10 still needed the most work, because it was the one that got at what this all meant, and so I had the most changes in it, finally throwing out a line that had been with me since the original journal entry and making the meaning of the title clearer by changing "chained myself with worry over expenses" to "always traveled cautiously, clinging to my luggage of daily obligations." Sometimes the changes are just for the sound, as in paragraph 8 where two sentences switch places or in paragraph 11, where two phrases reverse position. Retyped and a presentation text prepared, this is the version that was eventually published (see Figure 5.3).

# R *eaching the Final Draft*

Revision is seldom painless, but most often it is rewarding work. The original draft starts getting better before your eyes, perhaps richer, deeper, clearer. Often you need to go through the revision process again and again, starting with a global overview and working on the portions that demand attention during each complete reading. In the end, you have to return to yet another entire reading, one where the words and ideas on the page satisfy you enough that you feel it needs no more revising, that it says what you want it to say in a way that will be clearly understood by (and hopefully acceptable to) the reader for whom you intend it (even if that reader is only yourself). Only then should you worry about the quality of the presentation text.

---

# Traveling light, daring the world

Even though I was on my way to spend the night with friends in Grosse Pointe, I drove with the grim determination of someone going to a business meeting. It had been years since I'd traveled for pleasure, rather than for reasons connected with teaching, and I felt guilty leaving ungraded papers behind.

The red-haired hitchhiker in the passenger seat, a part-time musician I picked up on I-75 south of Flint, was cheerful and chatty. When we passed the Oakland University exit, I told her a college friend I hadn't seen for years was teaching there.

"You ought to go sit in one of his classes," she said. "It would really freak him out ." The thought delighted her and I smiled, more at her pleasure than at his possible surprise.

She hadn't traveled much lately, either. "Seems like I'm always living with some dude and can't really have a vacation," she said. But she took disappointment lightly, with only a few words of regret. "A friend was going to travel with me this weekend," she said later, "but his wife wouldn't let him. It's a real bummer." I nodded sympathetically.

She was headed for Canada for the weekend, with no destination in mind and only $2.35 in her jeans. I restrained an instinct to give paternalistic advice and asked how she could make it through the weekend on so little.

"Oh, maybe I'll get a gig in Windsor for the night." She shrugged. "Something will turn up." She was more interested in staring at the RenCen and said it really freaked her out.

I let her out near the river. She went off briskly toward unplanned adventure; I drove away toward Grosse Pointe, without the sense of urgency I had before on the interstate.

She seemed like a somewhat foolhardy, flaky flower-child, but she made me wonder why I always traveled cautiously, clinging to my luggage of daily obligation and responsibilities, while she could dare the world on $2.35.

Two weeks later I camped alone on the Leelanau Peninsula. I slept a few yards from Lake Michigan and strolled beach and forest. I even climbed the Sleeping Bear Dunes. They really freaked me out.

—*Robert L. Root, Jr.*
*Alma*

---

**FIGURE 5.3**   *Published Text*

In practice the final draft that emerges from thorough revision is, very often, also the presentation text submitted for publication or grading. Simply in the course of drafting and revising repeatedly the writer tends to correct as she goes along. But, also in practice, almost nobody can safely rely on the process of revision creating both final revised draft and presentation text. For that reason, the preparation of presentation text is best considered as a separate subprocess of composing. As with other subprocesses, to gain some objectivity and distance, the revised draft ought ideally to be set aside for a few hours or days before the preparation of a presentation copy begins. In the next chapter we will consider what that preparation involves.

---

**T**he Wordsmith on the Word Processor:

### Revising

Word-processing programs tend to make it easy to revise drafts, because the writer can move anywhere in the text and insert new language, delete old language, or replace language. It is also possible to keep a running record of drafts, first by printing out revised drafts as they are worked on, carefully labeling them so that you remember which is which, and second by letting you duplicate and/or rename a file to indicate which draft it is or what date it was composed. It is useful to compare drafts from time to time to gauge just how much revision has actually occurred. Following are a few more ideas for revising on the word processor.

**Alternative Drafts.** Sometimes it is useful to work on difficult sections of a paper by composing alternative drafts. Just as it is possible to write several widely varying openings to a paper and to follow up on the one that seems most promising, so it is possible to open up a new file and try composing a new section. If, for example, a description of an event seems dull in your first draft (maybe your first version described the event from an emotional distance, as if you were a reporter), try writing the description again, this time from a different perspective (perhaps with yourself as a first-person narrator, definitely there, definitely reacting or participating). Then use copy and paste commands to move the new version to the full paper to compare with the old section and to see how it works with the rest of the paper. You can create several alternative drafts of a section of the paper and try them all out in the full paper.

**Comparing Texts.** As we did with Melody's openings, use your word-processing program's column and page layout command to put two versions of a section or of the entire paper side by side to compare them and really see what you've done to change the paper. Remember that you don't have to change everything in a revision—part of what you revise for is to eliminate the weak parts without losing the strong parts—but if you compare two drafts and find only cosmetic changes (spelling, paragraphing, formatting), you may not have made substantive revisions. Some computer programs have special commands especially designed to let you do this side-by-side comparison on the screen.

An alternative is simply to open the files of both drafts, change each format so that each paper scrolls in a column down the screen (half the width of what it looks like normally), and then line up the open windows side by side. It will take some leaping back and forth among windows to scroll and to line up the beginnings of pages and paragraphs, but it will show you what has changed in those two texts.

**Sharing.** Sending your draft to someone else for a reaction is also helpful. The questions that another reader raises are often those that the writer needs to answer without realizing it. If your other reader is someone working on the same kind of thing you are working on—like a course assignment—just seeing what that person is doing opens your eyes to possibilities in your own piece. The trick in a lot of writing is finding a way to recognize the obvious (which is not always so obvious until someone else points it out or does something that helps you recognize it on your own). Many experienced wordsmiths use writing groups to gain some perspective on what needs to be revised in a work-in-progress; many composition and creative writing classrooms use them too. People who work together or people who are taking the same courses can also organize and benefit from groups. With the use of e-mail and various programs to send documents, it is possible to establish a writing group in cyberspace as well.

# 6

# *Going Public*

*I'll have the text as close to perfect as I think I can get it, will think it ready to send. Then the paper copy will expose how awkward and unfinished it is.*

—John Jerome

Up to this point I have been continually reminding you that composing is a recursive action, a jumble of processes and subprocesses that continually interrupt one another and work themselves out in a series of loops and switchbacks and rereading and reacting. In spite of the sequence of the preceding chapters—string-saving, prewriting, drafting, revising—I have been insisting that the composing process in practice is not really linear (or strictly sequential) and that any writer who tries to complete one subprocess before moving on to another will probably quickly become frustrated. Even the composing subprocess in this chapter—which I call "going public"—can be recursive; often the preparation of text calls for further revision of a sentence or a paragraph or a section, because you see the text in a new way.

But in the main I *do* want to treat going public as something separate from composing, to be done after the composing is completed. By preparation of presentation text I mean creating the clean, correct copy to present to another person, whether it is a teacher, editor, publisher, or potential reader of a self-published work. When manuscripts are accepted for publication, often someone other than, or in addition to, the author will be required to line-edit or proofread the work. For the publisher to make certain that the copy is correct before it goes off to the printer and for the printer to make certain the "proof" is free of error before running off hundreds or thousands of copies, careful line-by-line editing and word-by-word proofreading need to be done. Publishers and printers know—and writers ought to know—that good line editing and good proofreading take concentration and attention to the task and are most successfully performed when the person doing them is not simultaneously attending to something else. Concentrating on style and sense (the business of drafting and revising) distracts the reader from line editing and proofreading (the business of text preparation). *Composing* the text is a creative act, *going public* with it is chiefly a clerical task; the distinction is one between making meaning and preparing a presentation copy of the final draft.

## The Importance of Separating Text Preparation from Composing

The first reason for separating composing from text preparation is a practical one—if you do, you will create a better presentation copy. As much as it may be true that issues of written conformity in spelling, punctuation, grammar, and usage are not indications of a writer's powers of intellect or expression, it is also true that many readers are so distracted by nonconformity that engaging in conformity is worth the writer's while. This is particularly true if the reader to whom you're delivering the piece is someone who decides whether you will be published or paid or given a passing grade.

However, having a presentation text is also important for the writer, because the writer is one of the readers affected by the state of the manuscript. Composition teacher Elizabeth Bell, accustomed to writing on a word processor, found herself on one occasion having to draft and revise in longhand and was dismayed to discover how difficult it was to follow her own manuscript.

> I found myself frustrated by thumbing through pages of messed up, marked out, arrow-laden prose in search of a train of thought that sounded logical in my head, but appeared—when I could find it at all—fragmented and haphazard on the written page. (6)

The word processor, she finds, allows her "to see my work as a clean-copy whole, no matter at what stage of composing I am"; consequently she has a better sense of what she has accomplished in the draft and where she needs more work. She writes that "the process of being able to see and read one's work-in-progress without surface-level distractions can change one's relationship to the writing" and compares the discovery to her own experience as a writing teacher:

> Any teacher who has read stacks of student papers knows that the neatly written papers, especially if they come toward the end of the stack, enjoy a more kindly reception than their illegible, coffee-stained, more hapless colleagues. Whether or not the appearance of the paper ultimately affects our evaluation of the writing, it certainly affects the way we read it. The same, I discovered, is true of our own writing. Our way of reading our own writing—and perhaps our understanding of the purpose for doing it—changes when we are more immediately able to concentrate on its substantive levels instead of its accidental ones. (7)

If the state of the manuscript interferes with the reading for the writer herself, it must have a greater impact on a reader unfamiliar with the work.

John Jerome corroborates Elizabeth Bell's experience when he writes that "one of the more shocking events in electronic writing" occurs when he works on a printout of his draft. "I'll have the text as close to perfect as I think I can get it, will think it ready to send. Then the paper copy will expose how awkward and unfinished it really is" (111). The visual dimension of writing is more important than we sometimes realize, and clean hard copy helps us see past the surface to the substance below. By contrast, some word-processing features, such as variable typefaces and justified right margins, may be distracting even in correct copy; as Jerome says: "The writer wants the editor paying attention to the thinking, not the spaces between and around words" (125).

The second reason for separating composing from text preparation may seem to be less practical and more idealistic (although I would argue that it is equally practical): Writing ought to do the writer's business first and foremost, before it does anybody else's business. There may be exceptions to that rule—garbage disposer installation manuals and VCR operating instructions, for example—but in general the writer ought to write for herself even when writing something assigned by another person. At first glance, this may seem contradictory or paradoxical, but if you have not invested some portion of yourself in your writing, you are likely to produce work that is, at best, superficial, trivial, or perfunctory. There may be teachers—and undoubtedly there are—who prefer banal correctness over haphazard significance, but most prefer their student writers to make a commitment to the writing project and are willing to be flexible in evaluation to accommodate commitment. Moreover, there are real consequences to seeing a writing project as someone else's rather than your own. Connie Leas, a technical writer, has told of a writer she knew who put together an instruction manual for the United States Army made up of parts boilerplated together from other writing he had done. When military mechanics attempted to follow his manual to make repairs to truck engines, they found the instructions to be wrong, irrelevant to the kind of engine they were working on, and consequently they could not fix them (Root, "Writing" 160). The writer has to worry about how well his writing serves his readers, but he also has to have enough commitment to a project to understand what he is writing for himself. The two go together.

Composing, through all its prewriting, drafting and revising, is complete when the writer has discovered what she wants to say and has said it to a degree of development, clarity, and style that satisfies herself (given the situation). Going public is a separate action because in some cases it's an unnecessary one—you don't need to be published to have said what you wanted to say as well as you hoped to say it. Most practicing wordsmiths, no matter how successful they have been at writing, have accumulated a pile of rejection slips over the years. Only a relative handful of professional writers ever reaches the point where no one rejects anything they write. The experience of searching for a publisher teaches them that publishing is more often a question of finding a receptive reader than it is a question of somehow composing a universally acceptable text. Readers each bring to what they read their own backgrounds and assumptions; so too do editors and publishers and teachers. Getting the approval of readers sometimes requires waiting until the right readers come along; getting your own approval requires only working on a piece until it satisfies you enough for you to accept it as it is whether you ever go public with it or not.

## Preparing Academic Presentation Texts

Preparing papers for publishers and preparing papers for teachers may seem like quite different tasks—the person trying to publish has probably chosen a writing life, for one thing—but in reality the circumstances are very much the same. Publishers and teachers are both willing to provide guidelines for the prospective writer; both can be consulted about expectations for manuscript preparation.

In both cases a writer satisfies expectations more readily with each successive successful manuscript; having learned what worked in one piece the writer incorporates those elements into another and another until they recur almost automatically. Anyone who has waited for the first assignment in a course to be returned by the teacher knows the anxiety of that wait—this is the moment when you learn how well you interpreted the teacher's expectations, when you discover what needs to be done to adjust your approach to the subject on the next paper to get nearer to the teacher's expectations than you did this time. Since a good many academic papers are expected to be generally the same kind of paper, particularly within a given content area, most students can improve (with application) over a series of courses and teachers—the expectations generally aren't so widely divergent as to be unique to each individual case.

The basic rule of thumb in preparing academic texts is: *Always prepare the text as if it were assigned by the most demanding teacher.* If you try to satisfy the expectations of the most demanding reader, you will always satisfy the expectations of the least demanding. The corollary to that rule is: *Always work from the clearest possible sense of what specifically is being demanded of a presentation text by the person to whom you intend to submit it.* Academic journals usually publish the names of the style manuals they want contributors to follow ("the third edition of the *Publication Manual* of the American Psychological Association"; "the current edition of *The MLA Handbook*"); many publications will provide "instructions for authors" upon request; many publishers (such as Allyn and Bacon) publish their own guides for contracted authors; many teachers specify formats they want papers to follow and style manuals to be used in assignments—those who do not should be asked directly what they expect. A good handbook covering both MLA and APA styles usually covers most academic assignment requirements.

## S trategies for Preparing Presentation Text

Going public then is preparing a presentation copy of the final draft and submitting it to the reaction, recognition, and/or evaluation of other readers—editors, publishers, teachers, and other audiences. Consider the following as you prepare a presentation text:

- Plan time in which to prepare text as a separate activity. Just as with revising, set aside the final draft for at least twenty-four hours, having satisfied yourself that the content and expression of the draft are where you want them to be. When you read it to prepare a presentation text, try to read only for text preparation matters—spelling, punctuation, paragraphing, documentation format, capitalization, titles, pagination, boldfacing, underlining, and italics.

- Read the manuscript word for word. In reading for sense we tend to read in chunks of material, skimming sections and instantaneously surveying subsections, settling for the gist of a paragraph rather than following the sequence of words linearly. But the text preparer cannot afford to read as an interested reader. Reading word for word discovers problems of grammar and syntax, spelling, punctuation, and typing.

One good way of making certain you read every word is to read it aloud, particularly to another person. For example, read aloud this sentence from the second draft of the water-skiing paper in Chapter 5: "As the boat turned around to come back through, I was thinking that the speed the boat would be speeding up to was a speed that I never had made it through at before." If you hadn't noticed the repetition of the word "speed" during sight reading, you would during an oral reading, as well as the awkwardness of "never had made it through at before." You could then change the sentence to something that calls less attention to its syntax and more attention to its ideas: "As the boat turned around and started toward the buoys again, I realized that it would be taking me through at a speed I had never skied before" or "We turned around and the boat sped up, going faster than I had ever skied before." Either of these read aloud would sound better.

Writing groups often use this approach, allowing the writer to read aloud to several other people and letting their questions and comments guide revision or, in this case, editing. The writer takes responsibility for the proofreading. Often students who are having difficulty with text preparation discover their problems immediately by reading the text aloud. As in revision, so in text preparation the perspective of another person can be valuable. An alternative is to have someone else read a copy of the writer's draft aloud; the writer gets a sense of how the sentences sound and can observe the places where the reader has trouble following the text. A third alternative is to use a reliable friend, classmate, or relative as a line editor/proofreader.

- Read the manuscript with text preparation materials at hand. The text preparation materials would include a dictionary, a handbook of usage, any guidelines from the publisher or instructor, and any stylesheet or manual for documentation required by the project. Everybody needs to consult a dictionary or handbook from time to time, even people whose word processors have built-in spelling and grammar checkers. Guidelines from the publisher or instructor can change the rules by insisting on one specific documentation form over another (for example, MLA or APA) or simply by having their own idiosyncratic format (for example, one publisher insists that punctuation after underlined titles be underlined also, while another insists that punctuation should never be underlined).

- Read the manuscript for documentation separately from your reading for other matters. Formats for citing references are largely arbitrary, following no natural laws of language or usage; however, they do tend to be consistent within individual systems. The easiest way to make your documentation conform to the prescribed format is to perform a check of the documentation in your draft in consultation with the appropriate stylesheet or manual, as a separate action from the other text preparation you do. Identify the kind of citation you have and compare it item by item with the corresponding citation in the stylesheet, making yours conform to the stylesheet.

- Recognize that some text preparation problems surface only when preparing text, because text preparation is a clerical act, not a creative act. For example, in typing out handouts for my classes I routinely type "form" for "from" and "speculation" for "speculation." This kind of metathesis is not evidence of misspelling but evidence of mistyping, just as when my students type "the" as "tje". Knowing that I know how to spell "from" and "speculation" is not sufficient for my text preparation; I have to read text as if I didn't know these things, because they will surface in my final copy despite my knowledge unless I do.

- If you retype an entire page to correct some errors, reread the entire page, not just the place where the errors occurred. The problem with extensive retyping is that it provides new opportunities for error. The advantage that word processors have over typewriters is their ability to make corrections without extensive retyping of correct text, but even there it is necessary to reread. The word processor has created a whole new class of textual error, often caused by the editor's failure to delete old material at the same time that he inserts new material. Your local newspaper will daily provide examples of this kind of text preparation error.

- Edit and proofread from clean hard copy. Some people are very good at revising and editing from a computer screen, but many mistakes that show up in printouts are the kind not easily detected on the screen, such as misplaced or erroneous commands to the printer. Moreover, the end result is supposed to be clean hard copy, and it ought to be checked over as such before being submitted anywhere.

## **G** *etting a Background in Going Public*

Like so many ideas in this book, text preparation strategies are flexible, and no writer should use only one approach. Moreover, all of them assume a certain willingness to work at creating a clean, correct presentation text, a certain ability to recognize error, and a certain dexterity with reference tools. Not all writers can be assumed to have those talents at first, and probably those writers who do also have a background in reading published texts (so that they assimilate much of the information about what presentation texts look like) and in writing texts of one kind or another. For those who do not have that background, there are several ways of getting it.

- Read widely in the forms of writing you hope to or are required to produce. What are other people doing in this format? with this subject? for this audience? Moreover, how does the language of those people *sound?* Read some published texts aloud to yourself to get the rhythms of their language in your ear. Copy some of their pages word for word in longhand to force yourself to attend to the smallest units of their sentences.

- React to the text preparation of papers in writing when they are returned to you in academic courses. If you get back a paper where text preparation errors are noted, write a log entry or a journal entry about them, forcing yourself to analyze what they are and how to correct them. Consult a handbook or dictionary, a classmate or friend, or the course instructor, if the problem is not one you really understand. For example, one student wrote the following as part of a journal entry about text preparation errors on one of her papers:

> Each and other are two separate words that I always join together. I have to adhere to the concept of spacing between my words. I made this error in my paper: "Because Negaunee was a small town, everybody knew eachother." Actually, each and other are two separate words that should be written as such.
>
> A sentence fragment was pointed out on my third page of the draft. I wrote this: "Especially crabby mine workers who would come in after the midnight shift." This is not a complete sentence with a subject, predicate, and verb. I could correct this by adding a comma before the fragment instead of starting a new sentence. This is how it would look if I had done it correctly: "Customers sometimes treat waitresses in a rude manner, especially crabby mine workers who come in after the midnight shift." Sentence fragments should be an easy problem to correct, because there are many solutions to revising them.
>
> The only other problem I had was misspelled words, and I just looked those up in the dictionary.

Like other forms of writing, the act of writing logs and journals about text preparation problems is a way not only to solve them but to make you more aware of recurring problems and thus able to eliminate them more readily, perhaps more automatically.

- Create a checklist of the text preparation problems that recur in your drafts. If you have someone reading the text aloud or proofreading generally, note the errors they discover and keep track of them. If you have previous work with comments about text preparation on it—previous submissions or coursework from other teachers—review those comments and add to your checklist. The idea is to discover your particular recurring problems of text preparation and generate a list of items that you deliberately check either separately from or along with your other proofreading. If some teacher has highlighted your use of the semicolon, check every place you have a semicolon by consulting a usage handbook to see if you are using it as the handbook recommends; if teachers indicate that your paragraphs are generally either too short (one brief sentence) or too long (several pages), check your paragraphs to see where they begin and end and whether they could be either combined or broken up. Whatever the item that has gotten attention in the past, check for it in the present, particularly if it is one that has surfaced repeatedly. Constant deliberate checking for it may help eliminate it; it will certainly remedy it.

- Find an editor to work with you. It may be the course instructor, a roommate or classmate or tutor, a fellow writer or a writing group, a friend, or someone at a writing center. Talking with another person about problems you have had in the past and, in particular, about work-in-progress can help give you a better eye for not only what you do badly but also what you do well. Many scholars and teachers like to compare learning to write to learning to do an athletic activity, where individualized work with an experienced and accomplished coach can bring you farther faster than any textbook or series of lectures is likely to do. Just as talking to the golf pro or the batting coach or the aerobics instructor can improve your performance, so conferring with a writing coach can improve your composing. As your experience and skills grow, you will need that one-on-one consulting less and less.

Neal Gabler once commented that he tried to write his film reviews in longhand and save the typing for the final copy, as a reward (Root, *Working* 203). The reward of clean presentation copy is its neatness, its readability, the crisp black indentations marching across pristine white pages. Most writers have observed that published texts are even more readable somehow, but they have also observed that sometimes you don't spot things you could have said better until they appear in print. The advantage of appearing in print—or in typed presentation texts—frequently is that it trains you to spot things you could have said better earlier, before they appear in print.

So it is with careful text preparation in general. The more conscientious you are about it, the less you have to make corrections and changes. But it never becomes something that you can take for granted. Each time a final copy comes back to you, from a publisher or a teacher, review it not only for items they've noted but also for items you might have overlooked, then add them to your checklist. In time you will notice that the checklist isn't growing very much and that you run through it quickly. You'll also notice that there is never an occasion when you can simply accept your text on faith. Preparing to go public should be a regular stage in your writing.

## $T$*he Wordsmith on the Word Processor:*

### Going Public

Word processors have made the production of error-free presentation texts much easier than it was in the past. The marketing of word-processing programs often emphasizes the bells and whistles built into them to do text preparation chores easily, efficiently, accurately, even automatically. Yet, as helpful as they may be, the wordsmith needs to be aware of their limitations and never rely solely on cyber editors to prepare text to go public.

**Spell Checking.** Most word processing programs nowadays come with some sort of built-in program to check the spelling. Some are more time consuming than others, and few are so thorough that the writer can rely on them automatically. (If you have a spell checker that interrupts your writing to tell you you've misspelled or mistyped something, you should disable it anyway you can—text preparation concerns should not interfere with composing concerns; if they don't come automatically, they should come separately.) Often the dictionary in the word-processing program has too few words or too few variations of words. As it worked through this chapter, the spell checker on my word-processing program found some words I frequently misspell ("accomodate" for "accommodate", "committment" for "commitment"), but it also missed the boat on proper names (Connie, Neil, Negaunee), past tense and plural versions of words (curiously, it thinks "wordsmith" is correct but "wordsmiths" should be "word smiths"), and unfamiliar words (it recommended that "mistyping" be changed to "misty ping," whatever that means). Spell checkers are notorious for calling attention to proper names, and every time I have a list of references I know the spell-checking program will move slowly through it. One useful feature is the ability to add words to your personal dictionary, so that in future the program will recognize words it did not have in its dictionary originally. But many misspellings produce not nonwords but homonyms, words that sound the same—there, their, they're; two, too, to. Spell-checking programs cannot distinguish between proper and improper uses of correctly spelled words. You will have to look for these on your own.

**Grammar Checking Programs.**   Grammar checkers are aspects of word-processing programs that match sentences against a very finite set of rules about usage. Running this chapter through my grammar checker I found one place where I had made a mistake— I had typed "proofreading need to be done" and it should have been "proofreading needs to be done." The program caught that. But the program also raises many issues that I may not feel need to be raised. For example, it quarrels with both sentences from John Jerome that open the chapter, wondering whether they are complete sentences. They are, but usage guides tend to be very conservative and inflexible about what is permissible, and as a consequence they limit expression. Those sentences say exactly what Jerome wanted to say in exactly the way he wanted to say it—no error there. It is time consuming and potentially misleading to raise issues where the text is correct: My program asks me to consider using "are" for "is" in my own first sentence in the chapter, but "composing are a recursive action" is clearly wrong. Similarly, it asks me to think about using either "there," "they're," or "theirs" in place of "their" in Elizabeth Bell's phrase "their illegible, coffee-stained more hapless colleagues." Again, the program is wasting my time calling attention to a general rule that the prose hasn't violated. As with the spell checker, you should not rely on the grammar checker to catch errors in text preparation or to repair them automatically. You have to work with the text yourself.

**Text Preparation Files.**   One way of helping yourself out is to keep your error log on a word-processing file. This can accumulate over time, as manuscripts are returned to you and as you as well as others notice mistakes. Check the errors being called to your attention with your list of past errors and confront those that occur repeatedly. When you are preparing a presentation text, you can either print out your up-to-date error log or open the file to a window beside your text window, and reread your text looking specifically for the errors in your log. "Find" and "replace" commands in your word-processing program will also let you locate every potential recurring error.

# 7

# *Wordsmiths at Work*

*I deem myself to be an experienced writer because I have learned flexibility and the capacity for systematic variability.*
—Elaine P. Maimon

Libraries are rich in examples of wordsmiths at work. For example, *Working Days: The Journals of The Grapes of Wrath,* written by John Steinbeck and edited by Robert DeMott, gives readers a sense of the evolution of Steinbeck's great novel by recording the progress that he makes on it day by day. The book also reveals that, as systematic and persistent as Steinbeck was in the eventual full draft of the novel, *The Grapes of Wrath* came about only after Steinbeck had written a preliminary essay, edited another man's series of reports on migrant camps, and gone through several stages: a seven-part series of newspaper articles called "The Harvest Gypsies," an unfinished novel called *The Oklahomans,* a completed and then destroyed book-length satire called *L'affair Lettuceberg,* and the final work of his great novel. The book itself did not simply come out of him; it was preceded by immersion in context and various forms of trial runs. Immediately before starting the version that became *The Grapes of Wrath,* Steinbeck completed *L'affair Lettuceberg* and then wrote to his agent to explain why he had decided not to publish it. In part, he explained, "I had forgotten that I hadn't learned to write books, that I will never learn to write them. . . . I thought I could write easily and that anything I touched would be good simply because I did it. Well any such idea conscious or unconscious has been exploded for some time to come" (Steinbeck xl–xli). By that time Steinbeck, who was thirty-six, had already published eight books and was about to write his masterpiece.

**129**

Two points emerge from Steinbeck's example. One is that good writing is always hard, even for master wordsmiths; the other is that good writing, even for master wordsmiths, emerges out of a process of earlier string-saving, prewriting, and drafting, sometimes all jumbled up together.

I have cited an example of a novelist at work and similar examples abound, but examples of nonfiction writing are also plentiful. For instance, J. Lyndon Shanley's *The Making of Walden* is a fascinating study of the ways in which Henry David Thoreau drew upon his journals and other material to craft his great work, *Walden, or Life in the Woods*. Donald M. Murray's book *Shoptalk* collects a number of comments writers have made about their processes, most of which reinforce what has been said in the preceding chapters. In this concluding chapter I would like to give some examples of wordsmiths at work taken from my own classes in composition, in part because the processes of professionals are readily available in libraries, in part because these samples represent the attempts of novices to struggle at wordsmithery.

## A Wordsmith at Work: Writing about Growing Up

In the first example we get to see a student work through from preliminary explorations to a final draft that is thorough and well developed. The progress of a paper about growing up in his hometown led Brian through a number of activities, drafts, and revisions. He began with the preliminary work in Figure 7.1, a rough map of his hometown, and then a list of items the map helped him to recall about growing up.

In the course of making the list he discovered a number of memories about the local barbershop and decided that might make a topic worth further exploration. He used the barbershop as the center of a cluster diagram and let himself free-associate memories connected with it (Figure 7.2).

The clustering produced all kinds of memories and led him to make a list of what might go in a rough draft about the place (Figure 7.3). The questions at the end of the list help him to ponder what the point of writing about the barbershop might be.

All these preliminaries help get Brian back into the barbershop by drawing long-stored memories to the surface and immersing him in the experience once more. From this start he launches himself into a discovery draft, originally written in longhand.

ROUGH DRAFT

My Saturdays were always special to me as a young boy. I remember my Dad & I making the trip to Ink's Barber Shop. The day would basically start like all others. We would get up and have breakfast. About 9:00 AM we would either drive or walk down to the barber's shop. Everyone in the shop basically knows each other and says hi. It's sort of like when Norm walks in on Cheers—they all say hi. My dad & I would go in and shake hands and say hello.

**FIGURE 7.1** *Mapping and Listing*

Many things inside the shop were very intriguing. I remember the deer mounts on the wall. I would always try to get my dad to lift me up so I could pet them. The eyes of the deer always caught my attention. Whenever my dad was too busy to lift me up I would stare up at the mounts, until it was my turn to get my hair cut. I would walk all around the shop like I owned it. I thought it was a great place. Magazines in the shop got a great

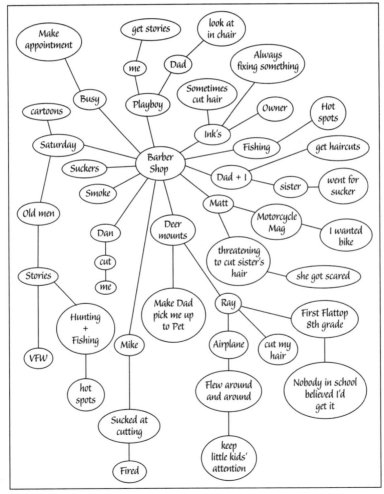

**FIGURE 7.2** *Clustering*

SATURDAY MORNINGS IN BARBER SHOP

Things in Shop

Deer Mounts—pet

AIRPLANE—get kids' attention

PLAYBOY—trying to get glances

MOTORCYCLE MAGS—dreaming

OLD MEN—stories hotspots

CARTOONS—on tv to watch

SMOKE—from cigarettes & cigars & pipes

HAIR ON THE GROUND

BARBERS    MATT, RAY, PETE (OWNER)

~~What significance does~~ How has ~~that~~ it affected my life?

What does it do for me? Why do I always enjoy getting my hair cut there?

Why do I feel at home there?

**FIGURE 7.3**  *Listing*

amount of attention from me. Matt, the barber who cut my dad's hair, always had motorcycle magazines for me to look at. I'd tell all the guys I was going to have a bike as soon as I could. I also remember Playboy. Being a horny little kid I'd walk all over the shop trying to get glances every now and then. The old men would read the newspaper or a hunting or fishing magazine. Since my grandfathers were big fishermen I always was all ears to a fishing story. The old men would smoke their cigs, cigars or pipes. I liked playing with the push button ashtrays. Pete Ink the owner would always come in to fix something and sometimes to cut a person's hair. Ray the barber who cut my hair always did a great job. When I would be running around he would tell me to stay out of the hair on the ground. Ray would always ask me how I wanted my hair cut even though I always got the same thing, every time. Ray had an airplane by his chair that he flew for little boys that cried and sometimes he would fly it for me. It would go round and round. I watched until I got dizzy. Ray's chair was also by the TV. So I got to watch cartoons too. They always had Bugs

Bunny on when Dad and I got there. The guys in the shop have affected me greatly in my views. They were always so nice to me and in return I've always been nice to them. Some of the old men in the shop would tell me stories of when my grandpa coached them in college. The barbershop always represented a place I could go and talk about fishing or anything else.

Brian lets his ideas tumble out of him in this draft and doesn't bother to paragraph or organize very much, simply letting the memories flow. In his next draft, also in longhand, he expands upon many of the ideas in this draft by adding descriptive details and also tries a conclusion that tells how he still likes to get his hair cut at Ink's Barber Shop. That draft he types up, breaking up the longhand draft into paragraphs and using the typed draft for more revision after discussion with group members in class about work-in-progress. The revisions are typed into that draft and a fourth version run off and handed in for teacher comments. When the paper comes back, a week or so later, Brian sits down and reads it through, then writes the following journal entry:

The paper sounds good and I like the story a lot. But now being away from it for a while I see a number of problems. The paragraphs that I have written need more details and to be broken down. Some of the paragraphs are too long. They go on and on switching from one subject to the next. I need to watch for this in papers to come. The main way the paper could be strengthened would be through details. The details would help the paper enormously. Adding to the motorcycle magazine will help put a picture in the reader's mind so they could see the bike I was looking at in the magazine. Talking about people in the shop, I need to give names to make them seem tangible to everyone. Just saying old man doesn't help. All you get with old man is a basic picture but using names invokes your imagination. Also to strengthen it would be to break up the paragraphs. This will make the paper flow easier and make easier reading. The main idea is details, talking about objects in the shop in greater depth. I need to paint a picture in the reader's mind with the details. Tell them how Ray's head looked before and after he got a hair piece. Tell the reader about the colors on the airplane by Ray's hair and how it worked. Was the plane loud, did it fly all over the shop or just in one place? Those are the kinds of questions I need to ask myself.

What works with this paper? I need to expand on ideas. Your ideas make total sense after a week layoff and then reading the paper again. I think the paper could be good but needs details. If I break up the paragraphs and add the details the paper will dramatically improve. The paper has to be a photo album in the reader's mind so they can see each and every picture in detail.

Having resolved to change paragraph structure and add details, Brian makes longhand revisions in his hard copy and then revises the paper on the word processor. In addition, he runs off a copy, checks it through for text preparation errors, makes a few corrections, and runs one last clean copy, error free, to include in his portfolio of class writing. The final draft reads as follows:

## Ink's Barber Shop

My Saturdays were always special to me as a young boy. I remember my dad and I making the trip to Ink's Barber Shop. The day would start like all others. We would get up, and I would eat my cereal in front of Bugs Bunny with my sister, Jill. If it was a nice day out we would walk downtown or else we would drive. The trip was about a half mile and did not take long. It was always fun walking across the bridge and running over the railroad tracks in town. It was nice to walk through downtown Kent.

At the barber shop everyone basically knows each other. The barbers would have their silk-looking shirts on and their barber licenses on the mirrors behind them. Now when I think about it, it reminds me of *Cheers* when Norm walks in and everyone says, "Norm." Dad and I would walk around and say "Hi" to everyone and get in line. People from all over Kent came to get their hair cut, like Doug Simms and his boy, David. My uncle Steve would drive my two cousins, Hugh and Ben, in to get their cuts. Ben and David were good friends and would play together in the shop.

To me as a small boy the shop had many temptations. The deer mounted on the wall always caught my attention first. I would beg Dad to lift me up so I could pet the deer. I would always stare at the eyes and touch the nose to see what it felt like. When you petted the hair of the deer it was soft and smooth. Other times when Dad would not lift me up I would stand under the mount and stare up at it. I loved walking all over the shop acting like I owned the place. Basically, I thought I did own it.

Matt, the barber who cut my dad's hair, always had motor-cycle magazines for me to look at. Looking at those motorcycle magazines made me want a motorcycle. I thought the sleek-looking race bikes were awesome. I would sit in the chair at the shop and pretend I was riding a motorcycle, revving the RPM's to pop a wheelie and take off. I would tell everyone in the shop I was going to get a bike. The other magazine I vividly remember was *Playboy*. Being a little kid I would wander around the shop hoping to get a glance of a naked woman. If I did get lucky and catch a glance, I could brag for a week straight to my friends.

The shop was always full of smoke from the old men smoking cigarettes. The old men would smoke and read fishing magazines or the newspaper. The shop had these ashtrays with buttons on the top, that would put your cigarette out if you pushed it. I would play with the ashtray forever just pushing that button over and over. While I was doing that the old men would tell me fishing stories or about playing football for Grandpa at Kent State University. I loved to hear stories about Grandpa or fishing.

My barber Ray also wore the silk-looking shirt and he always cut my hair. I would climb into the chair and he would ask me how I wanted my hair cut. But he knew it was always the same, nice and short. Ray always did a great job with my hair, cutting it perfectly. When I was running around the shop Ray would tell me to stay out of the hair on the ground.

I remember one Saturday when Dad and I went to get our hair cut and Ray was not bald anymore. He had hair on top of his head. I could not understand how he got his hair back. I sat there the whole time in the shop wondering how he got his hair back. It came in so quickly and was thick too. I talked myself into believ-ing that because Ray was a barber he could make his hair grow. Ray still today wears a hairpiece and it looks good.

Ray also had a real neat airplane by his chair. He flew the plane for kids that were scared. Since I thought I owned the shop I wasn't scared, but Ray sometimes would turn the plane on any-way for me. Ray's chair was also right by the TV so I got to watch Bugs Bunny while I got my hair cut. When I was finished getting my hair cut Ray made sure I got a sucker. My favorite flavor sucker was lemon-lime.

After Dad and I had both gotten our hair cut, it was time to pay. Dad sometimes would give me the money before we went in the shop so I could pay Ray. Dad told me to always give him an extra dollar as a tip for the good job. After paying Dad and I would say good-bye and head home to show Mom our new haircuts.

Ink's Barber Shop has left me with many fond memories. Whenever I go home to Kent, I always stop in the shop to say "Hi" or to get my hair cut from either Matt, Ray, or the newest barber, Dan, at Ink's Barber Shop.

The portrait of Ink's Barber Shop that emerges from Brian's final draft is affectionate and evocative, but it couldn't have been achieved without the preliminary work, the multiple drafts with their incremental revisions, the engagement with the writing through the analyzing journal entry, and the allowing for time in which the work could grow.

# A Wordsmith at Work: Writing a Research-Based Paper

Theresa's composition class has had a thematic organization. All the journals and assigned papers have made the students either focus on the role of popular media in their own lives or on the observation and analysis of various forms of media. Her earlier papers were about a speech she delivered, the kind of music she relates to, and the use of beepers or electronic pagers she observes around her. The fourth paper is to be based more on research than the other papers have been but, while the research has to be focused on media, it does not have to be entirely library-based research. Throughout the course she has been commenting in her journal on her course readings and media observations. When she writes in a log entry about the topic for her paper, she draws on ideas not only from her reading but also from her journal. Her log entry reads:

Right now I'm nearly clueless as to what I'm going to write a paper about. I was thinking of doing something regarding MTV's

"Singled Out" and the gender roles associated with dating, I may even do something about gender roles and romance novels. I'm interested in discovering how gender roles influence the dating world and how romance novels influence gender roles.

Of those two ideas she has already been doing background work on the former by watching the television show and writing an extensive journal entry about it.

On seeing gender in the mass media one of the most blatant examples would have to be MTV's "Singled Out." "Singled Out" is a dating show in which a contestant picks a date from 50 members of the opposite sex by asking a number of questions and elimination rounds. There is no middle ground on this show; it is either male dominated or female dominated. The males are dominant most of the time, partly because the more outspoken of the two hosts is a male. The entire show reduces dating to a sham and cover for baser activities.

From my point of view "Singled Out" reduces females to playing the role of the submissive wanton, simply a toy to be played with at the leisure of males. The mouthy male host helps to further degrade women with uncouth comments and rejoinders sprinkled in every now and then. The image the contestants themselves present strengthens the idea of the female toy. Females dress in flowery billowy dress, usually short (a throwback of the romantic Victorian) or skimpy, tight spandex or lycra outfits. These images cater to the male's ideal fantasy date. Men on the other hand come onto the show acting strong and macho, dressed in comfortable, everyday clothes, and generally not even hinting at sensitivity or intelligence. The females don't even notice the male brashness and lack of intelligence. How could the male fantasy be any more complete? The females are attractive (I feel they look sleazy, but who am I to say?), uncaring as to the males' overall appearance or personality, and thinking only of the no-strings-attached fling.

The image is further defined when one watches the actual competition. When a male "singles out" one of fifty women he does so with confidence and amusement, simply disposing of the ones he doesn't see as fit. (The first three stages of elimination are based on looks for the most part, so the male can create his own fantasy.) During the first three stages the eliminated contestants are marched past the male—it reminds me of a stockyard. The competition among females vying for a date also seems to be more fierce than that between the males. It is as if the male is the ultimate prize regardless of the male contestant himself.

When a female is the contestant doing the choosing she may exude the same confidence as the male, but not usually. Most of the females seem overwhelmed by the presence of so many virile men that they have trouble making a decision about which one to pick. The males who are eliminated also walk (I should say strut) past the female, seemingly saying, "Look what you're missing, but you're only one little fish and it's a big ocean." The males are not as hurt by rejection as females, if they are hurt at all. This is another element of the male fantasy—invincibility—the "I can hurt you, but you can't hurt me" way of thinking.

The final stage of the game also reinforces the dominant male image. Males sometimes express dismay at the date they've chosen, but females nearly always act happy and excited.

The journal entry is very detailed, and even though she wrote it mostly as a means of studying the topic around which the course centered, with no idea of writing a paper on it, she finds that she actually knows something about the subject. Moreover, she feels strongly about it and has observed the dynamics of the program very closely. She may not be entirely certain of the conclusions she will draw in the paper, but she knows she has materials and ideas to work with.

The television program is something she has confronted more recently and it stirs up stronger feelings than her alternative subject does. Her string-saving turns out to be an excellent resource for her. When she realizes that a local variation on the television program is going to be played in a university residence hall, she takes advantage of that opportunity in the hopes that it will produce some ideas, insights, or examples about her subject. She also goes to the library to see what secondary sources she can find. A week after her last log entry she writes another:

The topic I've chosen for this paper is MTV's "Singled Out" and gender roles. I believe I'm off to a decent start on this paper. I watched "Singled Out" for a week and took notes over the show. I also went to a mock "Singled Out" at Saxe-Herrig Hall. I've found some info in a psychological journal that will support my paper, but there were very few articles dealing directly w/ dating shows on TV.

She is immersing herself in her subject, rehearsing her ideas and language in notes, journal entries, and log entries.

The paper goes through several drafts, from as rough as the journal entry reprinted above to the much more polished, controlled, and carefully expressed final draft, reprinted below. As she goes through the revising of those multiple drafts, Theresa tries to apply to this paper the lessons she learned about her writing in the give-and-take among other student writers, her teacher, and herself over the semester. In one of her journal entries she discusses the strengths and weaknesses of her writing: "I have found that I have a strength in writing about issues that are emotional to me, but I always seem to have difficulty providing enough examples to make my meaning as clear and powerful as I'd like to." In particular she mentions how her progress on the "Singled Out" paper relates to her writing in general:

When I get a new assignment I usually have trouble with the very beginning of the paper. I never quite know how to set up the introduction. This problem varies from paper to paper. I've had more trouble starting my current assignment (paper #4) than the previous three. I think in order to correct this problem I need to start looking more closely at where I want my paper to go and what I want it to say in the end.

The recurring problem I tend to have with my writing is the problem of not providing enough examples as I mentioned before. For this next assignment I made a conscious effort to document examples of the behaviors I want to discuss in my paper.

Thinking about her composing processes and the reactions of readers to what she has accomplished in other papers, she tries to be alert to places in her writing where she has not been attentive before. In other words, she is making an effort to gain from the experience of her writing rather than treat each paper as a project for which she has to learn to write all over again.

She also makes an important discovery about the difference between writing about a personal subject and writing about an assigned academic subject. She writes in the same journal, "Another problem I am having with this current paper is involvement. I can't seem to make myself care about the subject matter. . . . My other papers centered around things I had known and experienced. I have never thought about, or been forced to think about, gender roles in a manner like this before this paper was assigned." Clearly from the evidence of her journal entry on the television show she has many thoughts about gender roles, but she has not had the opportunity or the need to express them or think them through this fully. The success of her paper in large measure comes about because, in spite of her previous lack of involvement in this subject, she is able to become personally committed to the work-in-progress. As she writes at the end of this journal entry, "If I can become personally involved with the paper it is much easier and much more enjoyable for me to write."

In her very next journal entry she discusses her progress on the paper and tries to add up what she has accomplished so far and what she needs to do in order to complete the paper successfully:

Most of my research for this paper came from simply watching the show. I was also able to find some psychological studies about dating and mate preference that may be of some use in supporting my findings. I feel I have enough examples of behaviors to create a solid foundation for this paper, but I'm not sure if I am presenting the information in a manner that grabs the reader's attention and gets my point across efficiently.

I need to get additional information about the film "The Dreamworld" in order to document it properly, since I am using the film for some background information. I was hoping to find current magazine articles pertaining to "Singled Out," but the ones I found dealt with ratings and advertising and those are beyond the scope of this paper.

I feel this paper has a lot of potential, but I'm positive it is going to need some extensive revisions in order for it to be what I want. While writing this paper I am trying to keep my opinions and feelings out of the text. I want the examples and the information presented to back up the main idea. I haven't really changed my writing style for this paper, but I may need to change the way I present my information.

These ideas help her focus on the aspects of her paper that need attention as the work progresses.

Finally, after several drafts, she turns in a paper that is considerably clearer, more developed, and more reasonable than the impromptu journal entry she first wrote on the television show.

## Dating in the Nineties

A film entitled "The Dreamworld" examined the roles of men and women in rock videos and how these images were detrimental to women. "The Dreamworld" found that women were exploited and objectified and always at the mercy of a controlling male. The women of rock videos were portrayed as wanting to be dominated and always eager to engage in sexual activities. The women who appeared in rock videos were generally dressed in tight fitting, skimpy clothing and were heavily ornamented. On the other hand the men appearing in rock videos were almost always dressed in a near normal fashion. Female video stars were shown as submissive by being filmed in crouched, kneeling or crawling positions. The males in video were always in control, of themselves and the females around them. However, music videos aren't the only source of these negative images of the female gender role. The roles played by men and women appearing on MTV's "Singled Out," a popular game show, reinforce the images presented by rock videos.

To conduct research for this paper I watched episodes of "Singled Out" on the MTV network, which is channel 13 in Mount Pleasant. I also attended a mock "Singled Out" held by a group of college students ranging in age from nineteen to twenty-two. The mock version was held in the Saxe-Herrig dormitory here at CMU on March 19, 1996. The behaviors of the men and women appearing on "Singled Out" correlated quite strongly with the actions of the college students participating in the mock game show. My findings regarding the television version were also very consistent from day to day.

"Singled Out" is a television game show set up in manner similar to that of "The Dating Game." The objective of the show is to "hook up" two couples by the end of the half-hour time slot. A female contestant "singles out" one of fifty eligible men from a "dating pool." Likewise, a male chooses a female from a group of fifty women. The show involves three levels of elimination and the contestants sit facing away from the dating pool. Prior to the show people in the dating pools fill out a personal profile based on questions varying from age and appearance to dating style and occupation. During the first round of elimination the contestants narrow the choices down by creating a profile of their ideal date. The members of the dating pool not meeting this profile are eliminated. By the second elimination the dating pool usually consists of six or seven people. This group is further reduced by the contestant asking each of the six people to accomplish some small, generally unusual task, such as barking like a dog or bowling with a coconut. The contestant keeps his or her three top choices, based on enthusiasm, imagination, and personal preferences to responses. The members of the dating pool who were eliminated during the first two rounds are allowed to walk past the contestant.

The reactions of the different genders varied slightly from day to day, but overall the actions of the rejected people reinforces the image of the submissive woman found in many rock videos. The episode of "Singled Out" that aired March 13, 1996, probably provides the best example of the differing actions of men and women. When the rejected women walked past the male contestant most had a tendency to walk in little groups and to avoid eye contact by looking at the floor or at the opposite wall of the recording studio. Both of these actions imply inferiority of the female. The men who were eliminated strutted by the female as if to say, "Hey, look what you're missing." Occasionally a female was brave enough to touch or kiss a male contestant, but the men were much more likely to initiate any contact.

The third and final elimination is based on the individual answers of the three remaining members of the dating pool to questions posed by the contestant. For every correct answer a person in the dating pool can move one block along a gameboard like path toward the contestant. The first person to reach the end of the path wins a night out with the contestant, paid for, of course, by "Singled Out" and its sponsors.

The manner of dress of the people appearing on "Singled Out," contestants and members of the dating pool alike, is consistent with the image of females examined by "The Dreamworld." The majority of the females appearing on the show wore tight, revealing clothing, generally form fitting jeans or shorts with bare midriff tops. If female contestants opted to wear a dress it

was low cut, above the knee, and made of a form hugging material. Most women wearing dresses also wore high heels to empha-
size the curves of their legs. I say only most women dressed in
this fashion because on every show there were a few women who
were dressed more conservatively, but the vast majority of
women appearing on the show wore clothing that forced them to
be uncomfortable during the duration of the program. They had
to stand ram-rod straight in heels, keep their bellies sucked in
and their chests stuck out to maintain their appearance.

On the other hand the clothing the men wore was considerably more relaxed and comfortable. Most men came on "Singled
Out" wearing loose fitting jeans and soft cotton shirts. The male
attire was just opposite that of the female clothing. The male
clothing was the epitome of comfort and leisure, while most
females had to make a constant effort to maintain their image.

The differences in male and female styles of dress are also
reflected in the appearance of the two hosts of the show. The female host, Jenny, always wore bare midriff tops with either very
tight pants or short skirts. Chris, the male host, dressed in baggy
clothing like the rest of the males appearing on the program.

The idea that females should be weak and submissive and
that males should be strong and dominant is further reinforced
by the events taking place during the elimination rounds. During
the first round a contestant can chose various categories by
which they can eliminate possible dates. Categories relating to
figure and appearance were prevalent among both sexes, but
dominated the male choices. Men were more likely to chose
categories such as "Figure," "Muscles," "Chest," "Hair Color,"
"Height," and "Weight." While females also picked from these
categories they were also the only contestants to opt for categories like "Commitment," "Career," and "Career Goals." Out of
the episodes viewed, one male chose the category "Commitment" and eliminated any female that was looking for a lasting
relationship. The categories used by the males to pick a date
were primarily based on appearance. Most men wanted a leggy
blond who would look good on their arm in public and who would
only expect a one-night relationship, further reinforcing the idea
that women are objects to be used only for their bodies and
appearance. The categories chosen by the women seem to give
the impression that they needed to be taken care of and that they

weren't capable of supporting themselves. These incidents further back the images of the dominant male and submissive female found in music videos.

At the start of the second round of elimination the remaining members of the dating pool are asked to introduce themselves. Of course they want the contestant to remember them, so they try to make their introduction as memorable as possible. This is an area where the differences in gender roles become glaringly apparent. People of both genders introduced themselves in a manner that implied they were fun to be with and were just out for a good time. However, there were differences in the responses of the males and females.

Males were more likely to give a response implying the female would reap great rewards by choosing them. A perfect example of this comes from the "Spring Break Edition" that aired on March 21, 1996. A man introduced himself by saying, "Hi, I'm Evan and I'll take you to heaven." During the March 13th show one male claimed "I know you want to meet me," and another introduced himself by saying "I want you bad." Another snappy male introduction came from the Saxe-Herrig "Singled Out" held March 19, 1996. One of the men responded with "You can pick the best or you can pick the rest." Judging from the way they introduce themselves these men must believe they are great prizes that women just long to have.

On the flip side there is the way females introduced themselves. Nearly all the female introductions dealt with the pleasure or ego of the male contestant. During the March 19th episode a female simply stated her name and then proceeded to tell the male contestant "You're all that" (in other words "You're God's gift to women"), and "I'll fulfill your every desire," was an opening line from the March 13th show. These responses are reflected in the non-television world. A female from the Saxe-Herrig "Singled Out" was asked what special dinner she would cook for her date. Her response was "Lobster because, well, you know." The tone and inflection she used to make this statement implied that much more than dinner would take place on the date.

As with any other game show there is interaction between the hosts and in the case of "Singled Out" this interaction says a lot about the role of women on the show. Chris is the primary host; he is the one that is in charge, and of course he is a male.

Jenny, the female host, does most of the actual work. She is the one that must walk from person to person in the dating pool with the microphone, while Chris is only responsible for dealing with the single contestant trying to choose a date. Jenny is also used to promote the show during commercials. During intermissions the show's announcer would say, "Stay tuned—there's a whole lot of Jenny coming up," but he never mentioned Chris. Jenny also is the target for most of Chris's sarcastic and sexist comments. His remarks ranged from comments about Jenny being grouchy "because it was that time of the month" (MTV March 19, 1996), or "she just can't control herself around all those men over there" (MTV March 20, 1996). The second comment did have some merit, Jenny was often very "touchy" around the men on the program. She would always stand very close to them, touch their faces, or run her fingers through their hair, while Chris very seldom made contact with anyone, male or female. Many times she appeared to be a toy there for the enjoyment of the males in the dating pool.

The interaction of the host and hostess of the Saxe-Herrig "Singled Out" was very similar to the MTV version. The male host was dressed in blue jeans, a loose flannel shirt, and tennis shoes. The female host followed in Jenny's footsteps, wearing a mini skirt and bare midriff top. The roles of the hosts in the mock version of the show were also very much like those of the hosts of the real television show. The male host was in charge of asking all the questions and making all the witty comments. The female host was once again the worker of the duo. She was the one in charge of taking care of the make-shift game board. During the Saxe-Herrig version the female host didn't even have a microphone, so more emphasis was put on her decorative purpose. There were many similarities between the dorm version and the real television episodes of "Singled Out," but there were also some subtle differences. The male host didn't make the sarcastic, mean comments toward his female cohost that are heard on the television episodes.

"Singled Out" is not the only culprit involved in presenting negative images of women. "Studs" was a short-lived dating show airing on the Fox network that also degraded women, probably more so than "Singled Out." "Studs" was generally set up with three women and two men. Each of the three women were sent on a date with each of the two men prior to the show. The show itself consisted of comparing answers to questions, similar to "The Newlywed Game." The two winners, one female and one male, were then sent on an all expense paid excursion as a prize. "Studs" was a very raunchy show. Often the winners were the ones who said the most daring things or implied that their date had gone farther than dinner and a movie. The contestants appearing on this particular show were very attractive people. The men were generally very well built with "good" features and the women were the usual long-legged blondes.

The images of men and women presented on "Singled Out" are not as harmless as many people seem to think. The television is a role model for establishing relationships with others and people are following its advice when it comes to dating; this is clearly seen by actions and responses of the college students participating in the mock version of "Singled Out." The tragedy of all this is that the images of women are those of toys and objects put on the earth only for the enjoyment of men. These negative images of women will continue to be reinforced as long as viewers continue to watch television shows such as "Singled Out," "Studs," and even "The Dating Game." As long as we continue to accept this behavior and watch these shows, women will continue to be treated as objects and toys.

### WORKS CITED

"Singled Out." Prod. Mark Cronin and Marci McDonald. MTV Networks. Burbank. March 13, 1996-March 20, 1996.

The Dreamworld. Dir. Sut Jhally. Amherst. 1991

In spite of her worries about not being involved with the subject, the final draft shows considerable commitment to describing, explaining, and evaluating the topic she selected.

# W orking at Wordsmithery

The process that a composition goes through may vary from fairly straightforward and sequential to bewilderingly convoluted, but the undeniable evidence of the testimony and texts of wordsmiths of all kinds is that success at wordsmithery grows out of commitment, effort, and time and can be fostered by an awareness of a range of strategies adapted to the needs of the project-in-progress. As these samples show, the final draft emerges out of a process of engaging ideas in written language, a process that is usually unpredictable in the ways language and thought interact with one another to produce drafts and texts, but a process that nonetheless you can direct and influence by understanding how they interact. Writers who know these things and make allowances for them are better able to appreciate their work and, consequently, better able to become accomplished at wordsmithery.

# Works Cited

Bell, Elizabeth. "The Magic Circle." *Writers on Writing*. Vol. 2. Ed. Tom Waldrep. New York: Random House, 1988. 3–10.

Bereiter, Carl. "Development in Writing." *Cognitive Processes in Writing*. Ed. Lee W. Gregg and Erwin R. Steinberg. Hillsdale: Lawrence Erlbaum, 1980. 73–93.

Couture, Barbara, and Jone Rymer. "Interactive Writing on the Job: Definitions and Implications of 'Collaboration,' " *Writing in the Business Professions*. Ed. Myra Kogen. Urbana: National Council of Teachers of English, 1989. 73–93.

Croft, Mary. "Pablo, Go Home and Paint." *Writers on Writing*. Vol. 2. Ed. Tom Waldrep. New York: Random House, 1988. 39–45.

Denby, David. Interview with the author. 14 Oct. 1982.

Dillard, Annie. "How I Wrote the Moth Essay—and Why," *The Norton Sampler*. 3rd ed. Ed. Thomas Cooley. New York: W. W. Norton & Co., 1985, 13–21.

Dillard, Annie. *The Writing Life*. New York: Harper & Row, 1989.

Dillman, Richard, Ed. *Thoreau's Comments on the Art of Writing*. New York: University Press of America, 1987.

Dowst, Kenneth. "The Epistemic Approach." *Eight Approaches to Teaching Composition*. Eds. Timothy R. Donovan & Ben W. McClelland. Urbana: National Council of Teachers of English, 1980.

Gornick, Vivian. "An American Woman in Egypt." *They Went: The Art and Craft of Travel Writing*. Ed. William Zinsser. Boston: Houghton Mifflin Co., 1991. 101–120.

Hampl, Patricia. "Memory and Imagination." *The Dolphin Reader*. 2nd ed. Ed. Douglas Hunt. Boston: Houghton Mifflin, 1990: 93–104.

Jerome, John. *The Writing Trade: A Year in the Life*. New York: Viking, 1992.

Lorch, Sue. "Confessions of a Former Sailor." *Writers on Writing*. Vol. 1. Ed. Tom Waldrep. New York: Random House, 1985. 165–171.

Maimon, Elaine P. "The Voices of a Writer's Mind." *Writers on Writing*. Vol. 2. Ed. Tom Waldrep. New York: Random House, 1988. 137–144.

McPhee, John. *The John McPhee Reader*. Ed. William Howarth. New York: Vintage, 1977.

Murray, Donald M. "One Writer's Secrets." *College Composition and Communication* 37 (May 1986): 146–153.

Murray, Donald M. *Shoptalk: Learning to Write with Writers*. Portsmouth, NH: Boynton/Cook-Heinemann, 1990.

Nykamp, Susan. Interview with the author. 15 Dec. 1982.

Olson, Sigurd. *Songs of the North*. Ed. Howard Frank Mosher. New York: Penguin, 1987.

Oomen, Anne-Marie. "Talking to Yourself in the Car is Okay: A Workshop about Writing Monologues and Dialogues." *Those Who Do, Can: Teachers Writing, Writers Teaching—A Sourcebook.* Eds. Robert L. Root, Jr., and Michael Steinberg. Urbana, IL: National Council of Teachers of English, 1996. 173–186.

Phelps, Louise Wetherbee. "Rhythm and Pattern in a Composing Life." *Writers on Writing.* Vol. 1. Ed. Tom Waldrep. New York: Random House, 1985. 241–257.

Plimpton, George, ed. *The Writer's Chapbook.* New York: Viking, 1989.

Polanyi, Michael. *Personal Knowledge: Towards a Post-Critical Philosophy.* Chicago: University of Chicago Press, 1968.

Primeau, Ronald N. *Writing in the Margins: From Annotation to Critical Essay.* New York: McKay, 1976.

Reeves, Richard. Interview with the author. 8 Nov. 1984.

Root, Robert L., Jr. *Thomas Southerne.* Twayne English Authors Series. Boston: Twayne Publishers, 1981.

Root, Robert L., Jr. *Working at Writing: Columnists and Critics Composing.* Carbondale: Southern Illinois University Press, 1991.

Root, Robert L., Jr. "Writing Trade Texts: A Career Writer Composing." *Issues in Writing* 6:2 (Spring/Summer 1994): 149–163.

Schneebaum, Tobias. "A Drive Into the Unknown." *They Went: The Art and Craft of Travel Writing.* Ed. William Zinsser. Boston: Houghton Mifflin Co., 1991. 141–165.

Schuster, Charles I. "Richard Selzer and John McPhee: A Contrastive Analysis of the Composing Process." Annual Conference of National Council of Teachers of English. San Antonio, 22 Nov. 1986.

Sommers, Nancy. "Between the Drafts." *College Composition and Communication* 43:1 (February 1992): 23–31.

Stapleton, Laurence, ed. *H. D. Thoreau: A Writer's Journal.* New York: Dover, 1960.

Steinbeck, John. *Working Days: The Journal of* The Grapes of Wrath. Ed. Robert DeMott. New York: Penguin, 1990.

Warnock, Tilly. "How I Write." *Writers on Writing.* Vol.1. Ed. Tom Waldrep. New York: Random House, 1985. 305–315.

White, E. B. *The Letters of E. B. White.* Ed. Dorothy Romano Guth. New York: Harper & Row, 1976.

Wicker, Tom. Interview with the author. 8 Oct. 1982.

Woolf, Virginia. *A Writer's Diary.* Ed. Leonard Woolf. New York: Harcourt, Brace, and Co., 1954.

Zwinger, Ann, and Edwin Way Teale. *A Conscious Stillness: Two Naturalists on Thoreau's Rivers.* New York: Harper & Row, 1982.

*Credits* (continued from page iv)

Barber, Theresa. Journals, logs, and final draft of "Dating in the Nineties." Reprinted by permission of the author.

Guizzetti, Mari L. Journal Entry 7. February 18, 1991. Reprinted by permission of the author.

Jerome, John. Excerpts from *The Writing Trade* by John Jerome. Copyright ® 1992 by John Jerome. Used by permission of Viking Penguin, a division of Penguin Books USA Inc.

Kerr, Walter. Notes for review of *Ghosts*. Reprinted by permission of the author.

Lundeen, Scott. "How I Gained Self-Confidence through Water-Skiing" (two drafts). Reprinted by permission of the author.

Pope, Mary Elizabeth. Two journal entries. Reprinted by permission of the author.

Powser, Heather C. Reading log on Jane Tompkins. March 30, 1992. Reprinted by permission of the author.

Rees, Brian T. "Ink's Barber Shop" (prewriting including mapping, listing, clustering; rough draft; journal entry on work in progress; and final draft). Reprinted by permission of the author.

Sagorski, Melody K. Journal entry and "A Report on Critical Reviews of *C. S. Lewis: A Biography* by A. N. Wilson" (multiple drafts of research paper). Reprinted by permission of the author.

Wargelin, Stacey E. Writing log: January 29, 1990. Reprinted by permission of the author.

# Index